Instant Vortex Plus Air Fryer Oven Cookbook 2020

Easy, Quick and Healthy Recipes for Smart People On a Budget

By Ashley Crawford

Table of Content

Introduction

An air frying oven is one of the most sought-after appliances because of its versatility and ease of use. The appliance will cook your food by circulating hot air into the cooking chamber. This is the best choice for individuals who are looking for the best fried foods without compromising its quality. In this book we are going to cover a wide array of cooking ways such as instant vortex air fryer oven. This is a 7 in 1 cooking appliance can perform seven functions of cooking without compromising the quality of foods. The air fryer is exceptionally good because it saves nearly 80% of your oil while frying your food. If you want to make French fries you will need very little oil. It is not limited to only the crunchy foods but also it is highly effective in cooking a wide array of foods.

You can roast a chicken, reheat frozen foods, bake muffins, and dehydrate your fruits as well.   The microprocessor technology utilized in the appliance makes it the best in cooking because it of the programmed keys. You can easily cook your foods without worrying about the time and temperature settings. Besides, the air fryer is vital because it reduces excess calories that is often associated with weight gain.   The appliance is made to ensure that you get high quality foods without adding more calories.   The crunchiness of the food from outside and tender inside is what separates it from the rest of the air fryers.   We have covered over 80 recipes in this book and you can choose any of the easy to make recipes and enjoy a meal at the comfort of your home.

Our main objective is to provide all the information about instant vortex air fryer oven to help you make the right choice.   Using this book, you will be able to cook tastier, healthier and fast meals within a short time.

Chapter 1 An In-Depth of Instant Vortex Air Fryer

Instant vortex air fryer is one of the revolutionary kitchen appliances that will help in making your cooking easy and simple. It is a sophisticated and a more mature version of the old traditional fryer and oven. The air fryer principally circulates hot air inside the vortex of the fryer and this is made possible by the vortex fan. This helps in making the cooking process faster and will make your meals by consuming little oil. The instant vortex fryer is a multicooker kitchen appliance that has seven in built programs. This means that your fryer can act as a multicooker as it fries, bakes, rotisserie, reheat, broiling as well as rehydrating the foods.   It is one of the best replacements for the traditional oven and grill, toaster and dehydrator.   Besides, since it is compact in size it will save a lot of space in your kitchen. One of the main benefits of the instant vortex

air fryer is that its expanded capacity of the f of air frying allows to cook a large quantity of food at once.

How Does it Work?

The instant vortex air fryer runs on a simple hot air technology which allows your food to be crispy on the outside and tender on the inside. The appliance comes with a LED screen display which allows you to choose various smart cooking functions. The vortex air fryer is a 1500-watt mini convection oven which is able to generate a maximum temperature of 400 degrees Fahrenheit. The appliance blows very hot air inside the oven and the convection fan will distribute the hot air to allow the appliance to cook the meal effectively.   This technology allows you to cook foods well and evenly.   The hot air technology is applicable in different aspects and you can fry your crisp French fries, broil burgers, or bake cakes and cookies. The vortex air fryer oven comes with an expanded capacity and this will allow you to roast a whole chicken at a go. Besides it can work as a dehydrator and you can use it to dehydrate your fruits.

The vortex air fryer usually releases heat from the heating element while cooking. It also has an exhaust fan located above the cooking chamber. This will allow to circulate air that is required to cook the food and maintain a fresh air circulation throughout the cooking process. Besides, it ensures that the air entering the oven is fresh and filtered to allow you to cook food in a healthier way. The vortex air fryer comes with 6 accessories with 2 cooking trays, rotisserie spit, rotisserie basket, drip pan, rotisserie lift and rotisserie fork.

Understanding the Functions of the Vortex Air Fryer Oven

The vortex air fryer has a touch screen LED screen that allows you to choose the function that you want to introduce. These functions are easy to key in and if you follow the guidelines in the book you will be in a better position to make high quality foods within no time. The functions are described as follows.

Display and touch panel

The vortex air fryer has a digital panel which makes your cooking convenient and easy. You can select the automatic as well as the manual function. The functions are easy to key in and you can change them until you have found the right function that you wanted.

Smart programs

The smart programs are automated based on the programmed functions. If you use these functions you will not need any time to set temperature or cooking time. Usually when the oven goes on standby mode it indicates

"OFF". the smart programs included in the oven include:

- Roast
- Air fry
- Bake
- Broil
- Dehydrate
- Reheat

Temperature function (+/-)

The temperature function will allow you to adjust the cooking temperature to the level that you want. You can hold the "+" to increase the temperature or the "- "to decrease the temperature to your liking. However, when you choose a program it will automatically choose the best temperature and cook your food to your liking.

Time (+/-)

This is used to adjust the time taken in cooking your food. You can use the '+' to increase the time taken to cook the food or you can use '- 'to reduce the time taken in cooking the food depending on your taste and preference. However, you can automatically choose a program that will cook the food at the required temperature.

Start

This function is effective in beginning the cooking process.

Rotate

This is a function key that you can use while roasting or any other process that requires a rotisserie. When you turn on the key the rotisserie will begin to rotate and if you want to turn it off you can press the same button again. This button is only available when you choose to roast or air fry. When the key indicates in a blue color it means that the rotate function is available.

Light

This function is available when you want to turn on or off the oven light. However, after 5 minutes of no activity the oven light will turn off automatically.

Cancel

This function is vital in stopping the cooking process. This is important especially if you have chosen the wrong function. When you press the cancel button the oven will go on standby mode and the display panel will indicates OFF.

How to use the Instant Vortex air Fryer Oven

It is imperative that you should follow the guide for you to understand how to use the oven effectively. Here is a step by step guide on how to use the oven.

1. First, you have to open the door of the air fryer and place the drip pan at the bottom of the air fryer oven and then close the door.
2. Plug in the power cord into the PowerPoint socket and switch it on. The oven will display 'OFF' on the screen and this will indicate that the oven has gone into a standby mode.
3. Choose air fry smart program by touching over the control panel. When the oven is in the smart program option the maximum temperature it can attain is 400 degrees Fahrenheit.
4. Press the Time (+/-) function and adjust the cooking time to say 10 minutes or 20 minutes depending on what you time you want your food cooked. When you are using the smart programs, it will save your last cooking time automatically.
5. Thereafter after pressing the time function you can choose select on the program panel to begin the cooking process. When the display reads ON it means that your oven is on preheat mode. You use the time or temperature button to either or increase any of the two.
6. Once you are done with the preheating process the oven will display 'add food'. this is usually a test run program and you should not add any food to the oven.
7. Open the air fry and insert both the cooking tray into the cooking chamber and utilize the oven mitts to put it in place. Close the oven door and the panel will display the cooking time.

8. During this process the oven will display 'turn food'. this is an indication that you need to turn your food during the cooking process. Open the oven door and the program will pause automatically. Close the door and the oven will resume the program.
9. The last time in the cooking process is often indicated in seconds and once the food is ready the oven panel will display 'end'.

Advantages of instant vortex air fryer oven

The vortex air fryer is the best option when it comes to cooking. You are looking at an alternative that will give you the best service while maintaining a high-quality food processing. Some of the benefits that the instant vortex air fryer comes with include:

Requires less fats and oils for cooking

Instant vortex air fryer will need very little oil and fats for your daily cooking. It will require 15% less than your normal cooking oil. When you fry a bowl of French fries you will need a tablespoonful of oil to make the most crunchy and tender fries.

Saves your time

One of the main benefits of instant vortex air fryer is that it will save you a lot of time that you will require to cook meals. It will blow very hot air into the cooking chamber and the food will cook within a short period. It is an ideal choice for people who have busy schedules and want to cook at the comfort of their homes.

Equipped with smart programs

The vortex air fryer is fully equipped with smart cooking functions that will help you reduce time and energy needed in cooking. With the smart programs you can just put food and the appliance will cook it optimally giving you quality food within a short period. The temperature and time are automatically adjusted to suit your needs.

Multifaceted appliance

The instant vortex air fryer oven is a 7 in 1 appliance which means that you can use it for seven cooking functions. The oven can bake, fry, broil, reheat, dehydrate fruits among others. All these functions are done by a single appliance and you do not have to worry about getting another appliance to do the different functions. Besides, you will be saving a lot of your kitchen space by purchasing the equipment.

It is safe to use

One of the main benefits of the instant vortex air fryer is that you can use it to cook without the fear that the device could cause any harm. When you are cooking food in the fryer it is closed on all sides therefore there is no risk of hot oil spilling or such injuries.

Protects the nutritional content in food

When you deep fry your food using the traditional deep-frying method, you are bound to damage the nutrients in the food. However, when you use the instant vortex oven you are sure that you are retain all the nutrients therefore you are sure that your body will be nourished.

Easy to clean

The vortex air fryer cooks your food using less oil therefore there will less grease on the cooking appliance. Besides the pan and rotisserie basket are essential in holding any oil and the cleaning process is quite easy.

Cooking Tips

a. If you are utilizing the rotisserie accessories you should place your food before you press the start button on the panel.

b. Most foods are given great cooking if you place them into a preheated oven. This is not applicable to rotisserie food. Once you have pressed the start button wait for the display to indicate 'add food' before you place the food inside the chamber.

c. For you to get crispy and golden fries soak your chips inside cold water for 15 to 20 minutes. After that time spray oil over the potato sticks before you place them inside the fryer.

d. It is always important that you flip your food when the panel reads 'turn food' this will allow your food to cook evenly.

e. To prevent splatter and excess steam injuries always pat moist food before you place them inside the oven.

f. If you want to season your food, always spray them with a little oil before seasoning them. This is critical because it will ensure that your seasoning sticks to the food.

g. While baking pie, cookies and any other food. It is better to cover them with foil to help in preventing any kind of overcooking from the top side.

Chapter 2 Breakfast Recipes

Breakfast Salmon Patties

Prep time: 10 minutes cook time: 8 minutes serves: 6

Ingredients

1 tsp paprika

1 egg slightly beaten

14 oz salmon, minced and drained

2 tsp green onion

2 tsp fresh coriander chopped well

Salt

Pepper

Instructions

1. Preheat the instant vortex air fryer until you attain 360 degrees Fahrenheit.
2. Add all your ingredients into a mixing bowl and mix them well until they are uniform and well blended.
3. Spray your oven with cooking oil or cooking spray.
4. Make 7 to 8 patties from the salmon mixture and put them on the pan and air fry them for 7 to 9 minutes. Always flip when the panel indicates 'turn food'.
5. Serve and enjoy.

Nnutrition facts per serving

Calories 122 Total Fats 5.6g, Carbohydrates 0.4g, Protein 16.5g, Sugar 0.2 g, Cholesterol 56 Mg.

Zucchini Fries

Preparation time: 10 minutes cooking time: 10 minutes serves: 4

Ingredients

½ tsp Italian seasoning

2 medium zucchini cuts into fries' shape

½ cup of parmesan cheese grated

1tsp garlic powder

½ cup breadcrumbs

Salt

Pepper

Instructions

1. In a shallow bowl mix together parmesan cheese, breadcrumbs, Italian seasoning, pepper, garlic powder and salt.
2. Coat your zucchini pieces with an egg then coat them again with breadcrumb mixture.
3. Spray your oven with oil or cooking spray.
4. Array the coated zucchini fries in a tray and air fry them in a pan at 400 degrees Fahrenheit.
5. Turn the food halfway through.
6. Serve and enjoy.

Nutritional value per serving

Calories 221.7 Fats 11.3g, Carbohydrates 13.5g, Proteins 16.5g, Sugar: 2.8g, Cholesterol:72mg.

Breakfast Stuffed Peppers

Preparation time: 10 minutes cooking time: 13 minutes serves: 2

Ingredients

Salt

Pepper

¼ tsp red chili flakes

1 bell pepper seeds removed, halved

4 eggs

Instructions

1. Crack two eggs into each of the bell pepper half and season it with salt.
2. Sprinkle with chili flakes on top.
3. Arrange the peppers on air fryer oven tray and cook them at 390 degrees Fahrenheit for 13 minutes.
4. Serve and enjoy.

Nutritional value per serving

Calories 168.4 Fat 11.2g, Protein 11.7g, Carbohydrates 5.2g, Sugar:3.7g, Cholesterol:327mg.

Crispy Breakfast Potatoes

Preparation time: 10 minutes cooking time: 10 minutes serves: 6

Ingredients

1 tsp garlic powder

1 tsp paprika

1 ½ potatoes diced into ½ inch cubes

1 tsp olive oil

¼ tsp chili powder

¼ tsp pepper

½ tsp dried parsley

2 tsp salt

Instructions

1. Put all your potatoes in a mixing bowl. Add all the remaining ingredients over the potatoes and toss them until they are even coated.
2. Arrange the potatoes in a pan and air fry them for 20 minutes at 400 degrees Fahrenheit.
3. Serve and enjoy.

Nutritional value per serving

Calories 173 Fat 9g, Protein 3g, Carbohydrates 20g.

Miracle Mom Simple Bagels

Preparation time: 10 minutes cooking time: 15 minutes serves: 4

Ingredients

1 tsp kosher salt

1 cup all-purpose flour

1 tsp baking powder

1 tsp water

1 cup plain Greek yoghurt

1 egg beaten

Toppings such as sesame seeds or any other seasonings

Instructions

1. In a large bowl mix together salt, baking powder and flour. Add the yoghurt and mix until doughball forms.
2. Turn out the dough into a floured surface and divide it into four balls
3. Roll reach ball into an 8-inch rope and join ends to form a bagel shape. Shape two bagels on each cooking tray.
4. In a small bowl combine 1 tsp of water and beaten egg. Brush over the tops and sides of the bagels.
5. Sprinkle toppings into the bagels and press lightly to ensure that they adhere to the surface.
6. Place the drip pan in place at the bottom of the cooking chamber and select AIRFRY mode then set your temperature to 330 degrees Celsius or allow the appliance to automatically select time and temperature.
7. When the display indicates add food, insert one cooking tray at the top and another at the bottom. When it indicates turn food, change the position to allow you to flip the food to allow it to cook on all sides.
8. Watch carefully and remove the bagels once they are rich golden brown. Serve warm.

Nutritional value per serving

Calories 305 Fats 5.4g, Carbohydrates 54.3g, Proteins 9.8 g, Dietary Fiber 9.8g.

Simply Bacon

Preparation time: 2 minutes cooking time: 10 minutes serves: 1 person

Ingredients

4 pieces of bacon

Instructions

1. Place the bacon strips on the instant vortex air fryer.
2. Cook for 10 minutes at 200 degrees Celsius.
3. Check when it browns and shows to be ready. Serve.

Nutritional value per serving

Calories 165, Fat 13g, Proteins 12 g, Carbs 0g

Grilled Cheese Sandwich

Preparation time: 12 minutes cooking time: 12 minutes serves: 1 person

Ingredients

2 slices of bread

2 pieces of bacon

½ tsp of olive oil side

Tomatoes

Jack cheese

Peach preserves

Instructions

1. If you have left over bacon from air fried bacon recipe you can get two pieces.   However, if you do not have any leftover bacon you can get two pieces and fry them at 200 degree Celsius.
2. Place olive oil on the side of the bread slices. Layer the rest of the ingredients on the non-oiled side following the following steps, peach preserves, tomatoes, jack cheese and cooked bacon.
3. Press down the bread to allow it to cook a little bit and peach side down too to allow the bread and the peel to spread evenly.
4. Place the sandwich in an air fryer and cook it for 12 minutes at 393 degrees Fahrenheit.
5. Serve once you are done.

Nutritional content per serving

Calories 282 Fats 18g, Carbs 18g, Proteins 12g, Sodium: 830 Mg, Potassium: 250mg

Potato Hash

Preparation time: 20 minutes cooking time: 25 minutes serves: 2

Ingredients

5 big potatoes

1 medium onion

2 eggs

½ tsp of thyme

½ green pepper

½ tsp savory

½ tsp black pepper

2 tsp duck fat

Instructions

1. Melt the duck fat in the fryer for 2 minutes and then peal your onion then dice it. Add to the fryer, wash and seed the green pepper to add a sumptuous taste. Cook for 5 minutes.

2. Wash your potatoes and peel them according to your taste and preference. Dice the potatoes into small cubes and add to the fryer along with the seasonings set the timer to 20 minutes and allow it to cook.

3. Spray a nonstick pan with cooking spray and grind some pepper before adding it in. let the pepper heat for a minute before adding your egg.   Cook until the egg becomes solid. Take the pan out and set it aside. Chop up the eggs.

4. Add the egg to the potato mixture once the timer runs out.

Nutritional value per serving

Calories 266 Fat 10g, Carbohydrates 39 g, Proteins 5g, Sodium: 5mg

Hash Browns

Preparation time: 10 minutes cooking time: 18 minutes serves: 3

Ingredients

1 tsp flour

1 ½ pound potatoes peeled

½ shallot

½ tsp Cajun seasoning

1 egg white

½ tsp black pepper

1 tsp coconut oil

Instructions

1. Keep the peeled potatoes in a bowl of water and mix them with Cajun seasoning as well as flour. Grate the potatoes and pour some cold water with a little salt to reduce the starch content. Set this mixture aside.

2. Grate the shallot and set it aside, strain your potatoes using a fine strainer or cheesecloth. Ensure all the water has been strained out of the potatoes.

3. Mix the ingredients in a bowl except the potatoes and ensure that they are well combined. Add the potatoes and mix them thoroughly. Form several patties.

4. Place your instant air fryer at 400 degrees Fahrenheit. Once the fryer indicates add food, add the patties on the pan. Flip every time the panel indicates turn food.

5. Serve while hot.

Nutritional value per serving

Calories 145 Fat 9g, Carbohydrates 15g, Proteins 1g, Sodium: 1990 Mg.

Latkes

Preparation time: 10 minutes cooking time: 7 minutes serves: 5

Ingredients

1 large onion

5 large potatoes peeled

4 large eggs

¼ cup potato starch

2 tsp kosher salt

½ tsp baking powder

Olive oil

Instructions

1. Scrub your potatoes well and place them in a food processor. Besides, place the shredded potatoes in a bowl of cool water and set it aside.

2. Rinse the food in the processor and grate the onions. Place your grated onions in a paper towel and squeeze out the liquid.

3. In a medium sized bowl whisk your eggs and add matzo, pepper, 1 tsp potato starch, baking powder and grated onion. Drain the water from the potatoes and save the starch that remains in your bowl.

4. Scoop the starch from the potato bowl and add to the latke mixture. Form latkes from the mixture in flat circles and dip into dry potato starch. Add oil and place them in an air fryer

5. Air fry your latkes at 360-degree Fahrenheit for 8 minutes and turn in the middle once it indicates turn food.

6. Serve while hot.

Nutritional content per serving

Calories 68 Fat 4g, Carbohydrates 6g, Protein 2g.

Eggs in a Hole

Preparation time: 5 minutes cook time: 7 minutes serves: 1

Ingredients

2 eggs

2 slices of bread

2 tsp butter

Pepper and salt to taste

Instructions

1. Using a jar punch two holes in the middle of your bread slices. This is the area where you will place your eggs.
2. Preheat your fryer to 330-degree Fahrenheit for about 5 minutes. Spread a tablespoon of butter into the pan and then add bread from the slices.
3. Crack the eggs and place them at the center of the bread slices and lightly season them with salt and pepper.
4. Take out your slices and rebutter the pan with the remaining butter and fry the other part for 3 minutes.
5. Serve while hot.

Nutritional value per one serving

Calories 787 Fat 51g, Carbohydrates 60g, Proteins 22g.

Whole30 Creamy Mushroom Smothered Pork Chops

Preparation time: 15 minutes cooking time: 18 minutes serves:4

Ingredients

2 cloves garlic

4 boneless pork chops

½ tsp ground black pepper

1 ½ tsp kosher salt

1 tsp finely chopped rosemary leaves

2 tsp extra virgin oil

8 ounces mushrooms

1 cup unsweetened milk

Instructions

1. Season the 4 boneless porkchops with ½ tsp black pepper and 1 tsp kosher salt

2. Finely chop 2 cloves garlic, 1 tsp fresh rosemary leaves and thinly slice 8-ounce mushrooms.

3. Heat 2 tsp oil in a pan and add the pork chops while working in batches and cook them until they are golden brown. Once done transfer them into a plate.

4. Add the mushrooms and kosher salt and put them in a baking tray. Put your appliance on bake mode and put the chicken inside the baking tray. Allow it to cook until it is golden brown. Add the mushrooms and cook them until all of them have browned well.

5. Add mushrooms and ½ tsp of kosher salt and cook for 5 more minutes add garlic and rosemary and allow it to add fragrance. Cook until you love your pork chops.

Nutritional value per serving

Calories 473.1 Fat 33.1g, Carbs 4.8 g, Fiber 0.5g, Proteins 39.0g, Sodium: 679.4mg

Easy Grilled Pork Chops with Sweet & Tangy Mustard Glaze

Preparation time: 10 minutes cook time: 45 minutes serves: 4

Ingredients

For the glace 1 ½ tsp cider

1 tsp Dijon mustard

2 tsp brown sugar

for the brine

3 cups light brown

2 bay leaves

2 tsp of salt

2 cloves smashed

1 ½ cups of ice cubes

4 boneless pork chops

Instructions

1. Make the glaze by placing all the ingredients in a small bowl and set them aside.

2. Brine your pork by placing it inside water with bay leaves, brown sugar, and garlic and heat it on medium heat. Cover and bring the mixture to boil. Uncover and stir it until the sugar is completely dissolved in the mixture. Add ice cubes to cool into it is slightly warm to the touch.

3. Once it is cooled submerge the pork chops and set aside for 15 minutes. Prepare your grill. Put the instant vortex fryer on GRILL mode and wait for it to attain the desired temperature. once it has attained 400 degree Celsius then it is time to add your pork chops. Usually the appliance will be indicated 'add food'.

4. Remove the pork chops from the salt mixture and pat them with paper towels. Place them on the grill and cover. Do not remove until they are well cooked. Once the instant fryer indicates TURN FOOD. flip your food and glaze it twice before allowing it to cook some more.

5. Transfer the pork to a clean cutting board once the appliance has indicated end. Serve while hot.

Nutritional value per serving

Calories 355.9 Fat 20.7g, Carbs 21.2g, Fiber 0.3%, Protein 21.2g, Sodium:1086.5mg

Chapter 3 Red Meat

Ultimate Beef Jerky

Preparation time: 20 minutes cook time: 180 minutes serves: 4

Ingredients

2 tsp honey

1 ½ beef round or any other lean cut

½ cup Worcestershire sauce

2 tsp onion powder

1 tsp pepper

1 tsp liquid smoke

½ tsp red pepper flakes

½ cup soy sauce

Instructions

1. Place your meat in zip top bag and freeze it for 2 hours to firm it up before cutting.
2. Slice the meat at along the grain at an 1/8 inch to ¼ inch stripes/
3. Mix the remaining ingredients in a zip top bag and add steak and coat it well. Marinate and put it in a refrigerator for 3 to 6 hours.
4. Remove the meat and pat it to remove any excess water. Divide the steak strips onto the cooking tray in an even layer with the texture and thickness of the grain being put into consideration.
5. Using the display panel in your instant vortex air fryer select DEHYDRATE option and adjust the temperature or allow it automatically choose the best temperature and time to dehydrate your meat.
6. After half the period that you have chosen switch trays.
7. Before the dehydration program is completely over, test a piece of your meat by bending it at 90 degrees angle.
8. If there is more moisture you can allow the meat 20 more minutes to allow it to dehydrate.
9. If it bends but there is no moisture then it is done.

Nutritional content per serving

Calories 367, Fat 23g, Carbs 10g, Proteins 30g, Sodium: 1870mg

Pistachio- crusted Rack of Lamb

Preparation time: 20 minutes cooking time: 25 minutes serves: 2

Ingredients

1 tsp kosher salt

¼ tsp pepper

1 rack of lamb trimmed and frenched.

2 tsp panko breadcrumbs

1/3 cup finely chopped pistachios

2 tsp finely chopped thyme

1 tsp Dijon

1 tsp butter melted

Instructions

1. Insert the spit into the rack and on the meaty side of the ribs closer to the bone. Use a metallic skewer to make the first hole if needed. Thread your rotisserie forks from each side and tighten the screws to hold the rack firmly in place. Season it with pepper and salt.

2. Place a dripping pan at the bottom of the cooking chamber and use the display panel to set the conditions that you want to use. Use AIRFRY and adjust the temperature or allow the appliance to choose the best time and temperature for the meat to be perfect. After the oven is set press START button.

3. When the display indicates 'add food' you can use the rotisserie tool to lift the spit into the cooking chamber and release the lever to secure the ends of the spit. Close the door of the oven and press ROTATE.

4. In a bowl combine the herbs and panko and drizzle on the butter before tossing them.

5. When the program is completely removing the meat and brush it with Dijon and press your pistachio firmly on all sides of the meat. Place the rack on a cooking tray this time the meaty side up.

6. Use the display panel and select AIRFRY and adjust the temperature to 380 degrees Fahrenheit and allow it to readjust before the panel displays START.

7. When the panel indicates 'add food' insert the cooking tray in its position and when TURN FOOD is displayed do not do anything.

8. When the air fry program is complete check your meat to ensure that the thickest portion of the meat is at least 140 degrees Celsius and allow it to rest for at least 10 minutes before slicing it into chops and serve.

Nutritional value per serving

Calories 611.8 Fat 39.8g, Carbs 10.3g, Proteins 53.1g, Sodium: 164 Mg

Rotisserie Roast Beef

Preparation time: 3 minutes cook time: 40 minutes serves: 3

Ingredients

2 ½ lbs. of top round roast

Garlic herb mix

Instructions

1. Put the roast on the rotisserie on the instant vortex air fryer.
2. Rub the roast with seasoning
3. Insert the roast inside the instant vortex plus and set the temperature to 350 degree Celsius and internal temperature to 145 degree Celsius. The appliance will indicate add food and this is the time you will add your roast.
4. Once the appliance indicates 'TURN FOOD' switch and rotate your roast.
5. Once the roast is done after 40 minutes, remove it carefully and let it rest for 10 minutes before slicing and serving it.
6. Remove the roast carefully. Allow to rest for about 10 minutes before slicing.

Nutritional value per serving

Calories 428 Fats 20g, Saturated Fat 8g, Carbohydrates 0g, Proteins 62g, Sodium: 148mg

Honey Sriracha Pork Tenderloin

Preparation time: 20 minutes cook time: 25 minutes serves: 3

Ingredients

2 tsp honey

1 lb. pork tenderloin

2 tsp sriracha hot sauce

1 ½ tsp kosher salt

Instructions

1. Insert the spit via the center of the pork tenderloin. Use a pointed metal skewer to make an original hole if needed.
2. Thread the rotisserie forks from each side and tighten the screws to hold the pork firmly in place.
3. In a small bowl combine salt, sriracha and honey. Brush over the pork tenderloin.
4. Place your drip pan in the bottom of your cooking chamber. This is important because it will help in maintaining all the fats and dripping material in place.
5. Using the display panel select AIRFRY and adjust the temperature of the appliance to 350 Fahrenheit and choose time to 20 minutes. Thereafter choose start.
6. When the display panel indicates ADD FOOD use the rotisserie fetch tool to lift the spit into your cooking chamber and using the red rotisserie release the lever and secure the ends of the spit.
7. Close the door and press ROTATE. Once you have flipped your tenderloin wait for it to be ready.
8. Once ready allow it to rest for 10 minutes before slicing it. Serve while hot.

Nutritional value per serving

Calories118 Fat 2g, Carbs 5g, Proteins 20g, Sodium :540mg

Dijon Rosemary Burgers

Preparation time: 20 minutes cook time: 10 minutes serves: 4

Ingredients

1 lb. of ground beef

½ cup of panko breadcrumbs

3 tsp Dijon mustard

¼ cup onion finely chopped

3 tsp soy sauce

1 tsp kosher salt

2 tsp fresh rosemary finely chopped

1 tsp brown sugar

Gruyere cheese slices

Favorite burger toppings

Instructions

1. In a large bowl, mix all the ingredients and form four patties. Place your patties on a cooking tray.
2. Place the drip pan at the bottom of the cooking chamber.
3. Using the display panel choose AIRFRY and adjust the temperature to 370-degree Fahrenheit and the time to 16 minutes and press START.
4. When the display panel indicates ADD FOOD, insert your cooking tray into the center position. Allow your burgers to cook and when the panel indicates TURN FOOD, flip your burgers.
5. In another bowl combine your sauce ingredients. When the air fry program is over checking the burgers if they are well cooked if not give them 5 more minutes.
6. Brush the burgers with sauce and top up with the cheese slices.
7. Using the display panel choose BROIL and adjust the timer to 3 minutes and press start.
8. When the BROIL program is over removing your burgers and serve them hot in toasted burns.

Nutritional value per serving

Calories 168, Fats 4g, Carbs 1g, Proteins 32g, Sodium:330mg

Sous Vide - Rosemary Leg of Lamb with Roasted Root Vegetables

Preparation time: 15 minutes cook time: 120 minutes serves: 4

Ingredients

For the lamb leg

2 lbs. of leg lamb

2 fresh rosemary springs

½ tsp garlic powder

For the roasted vegetables

6 carrots coarsely chopped

1 sweet onion diced

1 lb. fingerling potatoes chopped

2 parsnips peeled and diced

6 cloves garlic coarsely chopped

1 tsp minced fresh rosemary leaves

Instructions

1. Preheat a water bath up to 140-degree Fahrenheit lightly pepper and salt the lamb, then sprinkle garlic powder.
2. Place the leg of lamb in a sous vide bag and position the rosemary sprigs on the top then seal the bag.
3. Put the bag in water bath and allow it to cook for 3 hours. You should check to ensure that the meat is fully tender before you remove it.
4. For the vegetables, preheat your oven to 400 degrees Fahrenheit and then toss all the ingredients with olive oil then pepper and salt them.
5. Put a rimmed baking sheet and then cook stirring every 45 minutes until you get tender result.
6. Remove your sous de vide bag out of water and chuck the cooked leg of lamb. Dry it off thoroughly using a clean dish cloth or paper towels. Lightly salt it before searing for 1 minutes for each side.
7. Remove from the heat and cut the lamb into serving portions. Place the roasted vegetables on top. Add the zest of the orange on top and serve.

Nutritional value per serving

Calories 289, Fat 21g, Carbs 0g, Proteins 25g, Sodium:72mg, Potassium: 320mg

Pork Chops

Preparation time: 5 minutes cook time: 30 minutes serves: 3

Ingredients

1 cup butter milk

2 boneless pork chops

½ cup of flour

1 tsp garlic

Cooking oil spray

Salt and pepper to taste

Instructions

1. Put your pork chops in butter milk in a plastic bag
2. Marinate it for at least 30 minutes or as long as you like
3. Add salt, garlic, and pepper to your flour and mix it well.
4. Place the mixture in a plastic bag and add your pork chops and discard any extra butter milk.
5. Shake the bag until your pork chops are well coated with flour. Allow your pork chops to sit for 5 minutes for the flour to adhere.
6. Preheat your fryer to 380 degrees and spray the air fryer with oil.
7. Place the pork chops on the tray and spray them with oil.
8. Air fry your pork chops for 30 minutes until you see a golden-brown color. Flip the pork chops when the panel indicates TURN FOOD and respray the trays to ensure that the chops do not burn.
9. Once they are golden brown serve them. Enjoy

Nutritional value per serving

Calories Fats 4g Carbs 1g Proteins 23g Sodium: 210mg

Taquitos

Preparation time: 10 minutes cooking time: 10 minutes serves: 5

Ingredients

1 cup shredded cheese of your choice

½ cup diced onions

2 cups shredded meat

Spray cooking oil

1 package corn tortillas

Sour cream, salsa, cheese and guacamole for garnish

Instructions

1. Place your tortilla on a tray or plate.
2. Begin at one of the tortillas and place a small amount of onion, meat and cheese on the tortilla before rolling.
3. Place the tortilla on the air fryer basket.
4. Repeat until the air fryer basket is full. Do not crowd your taquitos.
5. Preheat your oven to 350 degrees Fahrenheit.
6. Air fry your taquitos for 8 minutes per side while switching or flipping them to ensure that they cook evenly.
7. Garnish with guacamole, sour cream, cheese and onion.

Nutritional value per serving

Calories 233 Fats 9g, Carbs 30g, Proteins 8g, Sodium: 310mg

Roast Beef

Preparation: 5 minutes cook time: 30 minutes serves: 4

Ingredients

pounds of beef roast

seasoning to taste

1 tsp olive oil

Instructions

1. Tie your roast to make it compact.
2. Rub your roast with olive oil.
3. Add seasoning and any other component that you would like.
4. Put your roast into the rotisserie or a tray depending on what you will use to roast your beef.
5. Air fry at 360 degrees Fahrenheit for 15 minutes per pound if you want medium rare.
6. Once it is done you can check to your liking or add a few more minutes to allow it to cook to your liking.
7. Let it cool for 5 minutes before serving.

Nutritional value per serving

Calories 129, Fat 3g, Carbs 0g, Proteins 30g, Sodium: 240mg

Greek Lamb Chops

Preparation time: 30 minutes cooking time: 15 minutes serves: 4 people

Ingredients

¼ cup olive oil

1 tsp salt

8 lamb chops

1 tsp olive oil for cooking

4 cloves garlic minced

2 tsp oregano chopped fresh

¼ cup lemon juice

Instructions

1. Using paper towels pat the chops dry and discard bone or shard fragments.
2. Mix all the ingredients together in a small bowl or jug.
3. Arrange the lamb chops in a large plate or baking dish and pour the marinade over the lamb rubbing it into the meat. Cover it with plastic wrap and marinate it for a half an hour or you can allow more time for a deeper flavor.
4. Besides, you can put your chops inside a refrigerator to ensure that the chops are in perfect condition to cook.
5. Heat your oven over high heat to allow you to air fry the lamb for 4 minutes per side.
6. Let it rest after air frying it before slicing it.
7. You can sprinkle a little extra oregano for an additional flavor.

Nutritional Value Per Serving

Calories 176, Fat 8g, Carbs 1g, Proteins 25g, Sodium: 367mg

Chapter 4 Poultry

Crispy Chicken Wings

Preparation time: 10 minutes cook time 30 minutes serves: 4

Ingredients

¼ cup melted butter

Seasoning

½ cup chicken broth

12 to 24 chicken wings

Instructions

1. Place your chicken wings into the instant air fryer. Add some broth.
2. Ensure that the chicken wings are well held on the cooking pan.
3. To maximize the functions of the instant air fryer you can prepare it prior to putting in some food. Press AIRFRYING and set timer to 25 minutes at 330 degrees Fahrenheit.
4. Allow it to prepare until you see ADD FOOD. once the panel indicates this, put your chicken wings into the cooking pan and insert into the chamber.
5. Press START and allow it to cook for 12 minutes per side. Once you see TURN FOOD. Flip your chicken wings to allow them to cook on both sides.
6. It is important that you have a drip pan at the bottom of the cooking chamber. Baste your chicken wings with butter and allow them to cook for another 2 minutes per side.
7. Once they turn golden you can remove them. serve while hot with a sauce of your choice.

Nutritional value per serving

Calories 214, Fat 14g, Carbs 2g, Proteins 20g, Sodium: 470mg

Rotisserie Chicken Recipe

Preparation time: 10 minutes cook time: 50 minutes serves: 4

Ingredients

2 cups of butter milk

Whole chicken

¼ cup olive oil

1 tsp sea salt

1 tsp garlic powder

Pepper and salt to taste

Instructions

1. Mix oil, butter milk, sea salt, and garlic powder in a large plastic bag.
2. Add a whole chicken and marinate it and allow it to sit for 6 hours. However, for the best results you can leave it for 24 hours for the chicken to take in the flavor properly.
3. Remove the chicken and season it with pepper and salt to taste.
4. Truss your chicken by removing the wings and tying the legs and around the chicken to hold it in place.
5. Place your chicken on a rotisserie spit and put it in an oven.
6. Set the oven to 380 degrees Fahrenheit and press AIRFRY. Allow your chicken to cook for about 50 minutes or until it turns golden brown. You can measure the internal temperature to a minimum of 165 degrees at the meatiest part of the thigh.
7. Remove the chicken using a removal tool and allow it to cool before serving.

Nutritional value per serving

Calories163, Fat 11g, Carbs 1g, Proteins 15g, Sodium: 620mg

Chicken Tenders

Preparation time: 5 minutes cook time: 15 minutes serves: 4

Ingredients

2 eggs

1-pound skinless chicken breasts cut into strips

½ a cup parmesan cheese

½ cup panko breadcrumbs

1/3 cup all-purpose flour

½ a cup butter milk

Cooking oil spray

Pepper and salt to taste

Instructions

1. Preheat your air fryer to 400 degrees Fahrenheit.
2. Put the chicken tenders in a zip lock bag and coat them with milk.
3. Mix parmesan cheese, pepper, salt, breadcrumbs and seasonings.
4. Put your eggs in another bowl and flour. Dredge the tenders through the flour shaking of any excess flour and dip them on the eggs in a bowl.
5. Put them on breadcrumbs for the crumbs to attach on the surface of the chicken.
6. Spray the air fryer trays and place the chicken tenders on the tray. Allow spacing do not over crowd them.
7. Spray the chicken tenders with oil. Air fry them for 5 minutes or wait until the appliance indicates turn food.
8. When this happens flip the tenders or switch trays if necessary, to allow them to cook evenly on both sides.

Nutritional value per serving

Calories 189, Fat 5g, Carbs 7g, Proteins 29g. Sodium: 320mg

Preparation time: 5 minutes cook time: 45 minutes serves: 3

Ingredients

3 lb. boneless breast

Brine or any rub of your choice

Instructions

1. Truss or tie the turkey breast to keep it compact in place.
2. Turn on the appliance and press AIRFRY, allow the appliance to prepare adequately. Once you see 'add food' option this is the right time to put your turkey breasts.
3. Air fry your turkey breast at 360 degrees Fahrenheit for 10 minutes per pound so in this case 30 minutes and turn it as much as possible.
4. The objective is to achieve an internal temperature of 160 degree Celsius and a golden-brown color.
5. Once cooked, allow it to cool and serve.

Nutritional value per serving

Calories, Fat 1g, Carbs 1g, Proteins 10g, Sodium: 420mg

Chinese Lemon Chicken

Preparation time: 10 minutes cook time: 20 minutes serves: 4

Ingredients

1 large egg

600 g chicken tenderloins cut into an inch piece

2 tsp soy sauce

½ a cup of corn starch

2 tsp of Chinese wine

½ a cup canola or vegetable oil

For lemon sauce

1 tsp of oil 1 tsp of finely grated ginger

3 tsp minced garlic

½ a cup chicken broth

2 tsp of soy sauce

2 tsp of honey

2 tsps. of sugar

Salt to taste

1 tsp of sesame seeds

Instructions

1. In a large bowl whisk egg, wine, and soy sauce. Add the chicken and mix well. Allow it to stand for 20 minutes to allow the flavor to sink in.
2. Put your corn starch in a large baking tray. Pour the chicken marinade into the corn starch and coat the chicken pieces evenly. Ensure you lightly press the corn starch around the chicken.
3. Turn on your air fryer oven and set temperature to 330 degrees Fahrenheit. We will be air frying therefore allow the program to attain the right temperature. Once it is ready shake off any excess corn starch and insert the chicken on the cooking chamber.
4. Have your draining pan in place to prevent damaging or dirtying the device.
5. Keep checking and flipping your chicken until it is golden brown and well cooked through.
6. For the sauce, sauté the garlic, ginger, soy sauce, stock, sugar, lemon juice, honey and a pinch of salt. Whisk and bring it to summer, keep cooking until all the sugar has dissolved.
7. Whisk your corn starch into the simmering sauce until the sugar dissolves. Toss your chicken and evenly coat with the sauce.
8. Garnish with green onions, sesame seeds and lemon slices. Serve.

Nutritional value per serving

Calories 450 Fats 18g, Carbohydrates 34 g, Proteins 38g, Sodium: 964mg, Potassium: 674 Mg, Iron: 1.7 Mg.

Crispy Lemon Garlic Parmesan Chicken Tenders

Preparation time: 10 minutes cook time: 20 minutes serves: 3

Ingredients

2 tsp olive oil

1 large egg

2 tsp lemon juice

1 tsp freshly chopped parsley

2 tsp minced garlic

¾ teaspoon salt to season

28 ounces of chicken tenders

1 cup breadcrumbs

1 tsp mild paprika

½ tsp garlic powder

½ tsp onion powder

¼ cup grated parmesan cheese

Instructions

1.   Preheat the oven to 380-degree Fahrenheit. Lightly grease the baking tray with cooking oil.
2.   In a large bowl whisk together oil, lemon juice, egg, garlic, parsley, pepper and salt.
3.   Dip the chicken tenders and allow them to sit for 5 minutes.
4.   In another bowl combine paprika, breadcrumbs, parmesan cheese and onion powder.
5.   Dredge the chicken tenders onto the egg to allow it coat evenly.
6.   Arrange the tenders on a baking sheet and lightly spray them with cooking oil.
7.   Bake each side for 5 to 10 minutes depending on the level of cooking that you want.

 Nutritional value per serving

Calories 379 Fat 15g, Carbohydrates 13g, Proteins 48g, Potassium: 788mg, Sodium: 888 Mg

Garlic Herb Butter Roast Chicken

Preparation time: 10 minutes cook time: 65 minutes serves: 8

Ingredients

3 tsp olive oil

4 pounds whole chicken

¼ cup unsalted butter melt

3 tsp olive oil

¼ cup wine

1 lemon halved

Freshly grounded pepper

4 garlic cloves

2 tsp freshly chopped parsley

1 head garlic peeled and cut in half

3 rosemary sprigs

Instructions

1. Preheat the oven to 380 degrees Fahrenheit. line your baking tray with a foul.
2. Remove any excess fat or left-over feathers on the chicken and rinse it under cold running water. Pat dry it with a clean cloth or paper towels.
3. Pour the melted butter, wine, olive oil juice and lemon over the chicken. Season the chicken liberally from the outside and inside the cavity adding salt and pepper.
4. Sprinkle over parsley and rub your minced garlic over the chicken while mixing all the ingredients together over the chicken under the skin.
5. Stuff the garlic head into the chicken cavity along with the rosemary sprigs.
6. Tie the legs of the chicken together before putting the chicken into a baking tray.
7. Allow it to cook for 20 minutes and baste halfway until juices run clear when you pierce the chicken thigh with a skewer.
8. Baste again and allow it to cook for 5 minutes.
9. Remove from the oven and cover it with a foil allowing it to cool before serving.

Nutritional content per serving.

Calories 579 Fat 31g, Carbohydrates 4g, Proteins 71g, Sodium: 195 Mg, Potassium: 588mg

Hummus-Crusted Chicken

Preparation time: 5 minutes cook time: 25 minutes serves: 4

Ingredients

4 boneless skinless, chicken breasts

1 tsp kosher salt

Cooking spray

¼ tsp freshly ground pepper

¼ cup hummus

½ tsp smoked paprika

Instructions

1. Arrange a rack in the middle of your oven and set it to 400 degrees Fahrenheit. lightly grease your baking sheet with a cooking spray.
2. Dry your chicken on all sides with paper towels and season with pepper and salt.
3. Arrange your chicken in a single layer on a baking sheet and spread the hummus over the chicken. Spread into a thin layer until each chicken breast is evenly coated. Sprinkle paprika over the hummus.
4. Bake the chicken until it is completely cooked through the temperature should be around 165 degrees Fahrenheit.
5. Turn the appliance into BROIL and cook the chicken until the hummus is dry to touch and browned. Serve it immediately.

Nutritional value per serving

Calories Fat 11.7g, Carbs 3.3g, Proteins 62.5g, Sodium: 653.6mg

Preparation 15 minutes cook time: 12 serves: 4

Ingredients

1 large thinly sliced onion

2 tsp olive oil

1 tsp kosher salt

2 large red bell papers thinly sliced

1 medium jalapeno sliced

4 cloves garlic

1 ½ boneless

1 tsp dried oregano

1 tsp ground cumin

2 tsp freshly squeezed lime juice

Lemon wedges

Instructions

1. Cook the onions by heating a tablespoon of oil in a pan over medium heat until simmering. Add onions and season it with ¼ tsp of salt to taste. Cook, often tossing with tongs until they brown.

2. Cook the jalapenos, peppers and garlic until they are fragrant. Add jalapeno, bell peppers and garlic and season with salt. Toss them until they are fragrant.

3. Brown your chicken with spices and transfer the vegetables to a plate. Put your pan to medium high and add the remaining tablespoon of oil. Add the chicken and season with oregano, cumin, ½ teaspoon salt. Cook the chicken until it is golden brown in color. use the BAKE mode on the fryer to give you the best taste and cooking.

4. Add vegetables to your baking pan and finish the cooking. Cook until the chicken is tender and serve the chicken, vegetables in warm tortillas.

5. You can add vegetables and sour cream to taste.

Nutritional value per serving

Calories 233, Fat 5g, Carbs 18g, Proteins 29g, Sodium: 379 Mg

General Tso's Chicken

Preparation time: 15 minutes cooking time: 15 minutes serves: 4

Ingredients

Ingredients

2 tsp hoisin sauce

1 tsp rice vinegar

¼ cup low sodium chicken broth

1 tsp toasted sesame

¼ cup cornstarch

¼ tsp red pepper flakes

½ tsp ground ginger

3 tsp vegetable oil

3 medium scallions

Cooked white rice

Instructions

1. To make the sauce, whisk broth, hoisin sauce, soy sauce, vinegar, sesame oil, ginger, 1 tsp cornstarch, and red pepper flakes together in a bowl and set it aside.

2. Season and coat the chicken with cornstarch. Put the chicken in a medium bowl and toss it with your hands until it is evenly coated. Ensure that there are no chicken wings that are stuck together.

3. Sear your chicken in two batches. Heat 2 tsp of oil in a pan over medium high heat. Add the chicken and put your appliance to BAKE mode and put them in a baking tray. Once you have added the chicken to the baking tray ensure to put a tray below to collect any oil that might pass through.

4. Cooking the chicken until it is golden brown or the instant air fryer indicates 'turn food', flip the chicken to ensure that it is well cooked. Add scallions and return it to the oven and bake it some few minutes to allow the flavor to fuse.

5. Add the sauce and serve while hot.

Nutritional value per serving

Calories 377.1 Fat 19.1g, Carbohydrates 16.4g, Proteins 34.9g, Sodium: 556.3mg

Air Fryer Fried Chicken

Preparation time: 8 minutes cook time: 50 minutes serves: 6

Ingredients

2 cups buttermilk

1 tsp freshly grounded pepper

1 whole chicken

2 cups all-purpose flour

2 tsp paprika

1 tsp garlic powder 1 tsp cayenne pepper

1 tsp ground mustard

Cooking spray

Instructions

1. Cut your chicken into 10 pieces. Place the pieces in a large bowl and season with 1 tsp of kosher salt and pepper. Add 2 cups of butter milk and marinate for at least 1 hour.

2. Meanwhile whisk the remaining 1 tsp kosher salt, 2 cups all-purpose flour, 1 tsp garlic powder, 2 tsp paprika, 1 tsp onion powder, 1 tsp cayenne pepper, 1 tsp ground mustard in a large bowl.

3. Preheat your instant vortex air plus to 390 degrees Fahrenheit.   Coat the air fryer with cooking spray, remove the chicken from butter milk and allow any excess to drip off.

4. Dredge your chicken in the flour mixture and shake of the excess flour on the chicken. Place a single chicken on the basket and give space between the pieces. On the AIRFRY mode once the appliance indicates TURN FOOD, flip your chicken breasts and allow them to cook for another 20 minutes.

5. Repeat with the remaining chicken and serve them while hot with a sauce of your choice.

Nutritional value per serving

Calories 1057 Fat 76g, Carbohydrates 52.1g, Proteins 41.7g, Sodium:1056mg

Peruvian Roasted Chicken with Green Sauce

Preparation time: 10 minutes cook time: 30 minutes serves: 4

Ingredients

3 cloves garlic minced

¼ cup freshly squeezed lime juice

3 tsp olive oil

1 tsp paprika

1 tsp cumin

1 tsp kosher salt

½ tsp dried oregano

½ tsp black pepper

2 pounds of chicken thighs

For the sauce

1/3 cup whole milk

1 cup cilantro leave

2 ounces feta cheese

2 medium jalapenos

½ tsp kosher salt

1 clove garlic 1 tsp extra virgin oil

Instructions

1. Combine cumin, olive oil, lime juice, paprika, pepper, salt and oregano in a large bowl. Add the chicken thighs and shake them to ensure that they are evenly coated. Give it time to ensure that it is highly effective.

2. Put your instant fryer on BAKE mode and you have to choose start and allow it to attain 425 degrees Fahrenheit to get the best.

3. Remove the chicken from the marinade and shake the excess marinade and arrange the chicken on a baking dish. Roast them until the chicken is half through. You will be able to flip them and change to ensure that it is cooked on the other side.

4. Meanwhile prepare the green sauce by placing all the ingredients in a food processor and blend until they are smooth. When the chicken is ready, turn on the broiler and add allow the chicken to turn crispy and serve it with the green sauce.

Nutritional value per serving

Calories 624.7 Fats 50.3g, Carbohydrates 6.9g, Proteins 36.1g, Fiber 1.1g, Sodium 641.7mg

Chapter 5 Fish and Seafood

Coconut Shrimp

Preparation time: 15 minutes cook time: 15 minutes serves :4

Ingredients

1-pound jumbo shrimp peeled

½ cup all-purpose flour

Salt and pepper

For batter

½ a cup all-purpose flour

1 tsp baking powder

1 egg

½ tsp garlic powder

1 cup breadcrumbs

1 cup shredded coconut

Instructions

1. Line your baking pan with a sheet or parchment paper.
2. On a shallow bout add ½ a cup of flour for dredging and in another bowl whish all ingredients together and it should resemble a pan cake consistency. Add a little mineral water or beer if it is too thick.
3. Dredge in the flour and shake off any excess four before coating with the breadcrumb and coconut mixture.
4. Lightly press the coconut into the shrimp.
5. Place in a prepared baking sheet and repeat the process for all the remaining shrimp.
6. Put your appliance on AIRFRY mode, once it is ready put the shrimp inside the cooking chamber. Arrange the shrimp well and ensure that they are well cooked.
7. Once cooked serve immediately with sweet chili sauce.

Nutritional value per serving

Calories 403, Fat 11g, Carbohydrates 46g, Proteins 30g, Potassium: 345mg, Sodium: 767mg

Baked Salmon with Butter Cream Sauce

Preparation time: 10 minutes cook time: 30 minutes serves: 2

Ingredients

4 skinless salmon fillets

1 tsp olive oil

1 tsp minced garlic

2 tsp dry white whine

Salt to season

Pepper

For lemon butter cream sauce

2 tsp minced garlic

¼ cup unsalted butter

2 tsp dry white wine

½ a cup heavy cream

1 cup freshly squeezed lemon

Instructions

1. Heat the oven to 380 degrees Fahrenheit and lightly grease your baking dish.
2. Pat the salmon to ensure that it is dry.
3. Combine olive oil, lemon juice, garlic and wine together in a small bowl. Rub the salmon with the mixture and arrange them in a baking dish. Season it with a good pinch of salt.
4. Bake for 10 minutes until the salmon is browned. Add garlic and bake for 20 seconds for the flavor to infuse.
5. Pour the wine and allow it to cook for 3 minutes.
6. Pour sauce over the cooked salmon and mix them with naturally released to baking tray.
7. Serve while hot.

Nutritional content per serving

Calories 254, Fat 26g, Carbohydrates 4g, Proteins 1g. Potassium: 47mg, Sodium: 16mg

Butter Seared Lobster Tails

Preparation time: 10 minutes cooking time: 15 minutes serves: 2

Ingredients

170 grams lobster tails

1 tsp to taste

2 tsp cooking oil

1 tsp salt to taste

4 cloves garlic crushed

Lemon slice

2 tsp fresh lemon juice

1 tsp parsley to garnish

Instructions

1. Thaw your lobster tails if they are frozen in a pot of cold water for an hour. Ensure that the lobster tails are fully thawed.
2. Rinse them and pat dry with paper towels.
3. Using a sharp knife or kitchen shears cut the top shell down through the center of the back of the end of the tail but leaving the tail intact. Remove the shell shards and run your finger between the shell and the meat.
4. Make sure that you are careful not to pull the tail out. Season your lobsters generously with pepper and salt.
5. Heat 2 tsp of oil and butter in a pan or skillet depending on what you are using. Swirl a tablespoonful of lemon juice and shear your lobster flesh side on the pan for 2 minutes until they are golden and crispy.
6. Flip the lobster tails, cover your pan and let it cook for 2 minutes until they are ink or the meat has cooked through.
7. Melt the remaining butter inside a skillet and sauté garlic until they are fragrant. squeeze the remaining lemon juice and spoon the juices over the lobster meat.
8. Turn off the heat immediately and garnish your lobsters with parsley.
9. Serve your lobsters with the remaining lemon slices and pan sauce.

Nutritional value per serving

Calories 368 Fats 28g, Carbohydrates 1g, Proteins 28g, Sodium: 390mg

Creamy Salmon Piccata

Preparation time: 5 minutes cook time: 40 minutes serves: 2

Ingredients

6 oz skinless salmon fillets

¼ cup flour

2 tsp unsalted butter

1/3 cup dry white wine

1 tsp olive oil

4 medium garlic cloves minced

1 cup low sodium chicken broth

2 tsp cornstarch

4 tsp fresh lemon juice

4 tsp parsley coarsely chopped

½ cup reduced fat cream

Lemon slices

Instructions

1. Season both sides of your salmon fillets evenly with pepper and salt. Add ¼ cup of flour to the dish and dredge the salmon in the flour to evenly coat it. Shake off the excess flour.

2. Melt 1 tsp of butter in a large skillet over medium heat. Add a tablespoonful of oil and swill to mix through butter. Add your salmon and sauté 4 minutes each side. Transfer your salmon into a warm plate and tent it with foil.

3. Add a teaspoonful of oil or butter and melt it. Add your garlic and sauté it until the fragrance seeps in, add the white wine and bring it to boil scrapping any bits on the pan.

4. Cook until the liquid is almost over in the pan and stir occasionally to ensure that it does not stick to the pan. Add ¾ cup of the broth and lemon juice before bringing it to boil and cook it for another minutes.

5. Mix 2 tablespoonful of broth and cornstarch whisking them well to ensure that it is well mixed. Pour the mixture into a pan and stir the liquid to make sauce. If the thickness is not pleasing to you add more cornstarch. Stir in the cream and remove from the heat and add your cappers.

6. Place your salmon fillet back into the pan and sprinkle pepper, chopped parsley and the lemon slices.

7. Serve the food immediately over rice and sauce or vegetables and plaster with a salad.

Nutritional value per serving

Calories Fats 25g, Carbohydrates 13 G, Proteins 38g, Sodium: 526mg, Potassium: 1018mg, Calcium: 76mg

Garlic Butter Baked Salmon

Preparation time: 10 minutes cook time: 25 minutes serves: 3

Ingredients

2 tsp olive oil

1 ½ tsp salt

1-pound baby potatoes

3 bunches of asparagus

½ cup melted unsalted butter

1/3 cup freshly squeezed lemon juice

2 ½ tsp minced garlic

6 oz skinless salmon fillets

1 lemon for garnishing

2 tsp dry white wine

Instructions

1. Heat the oven and set it to 380-degree Fahrenheit. On a large baking sheet toss together your potatoes with oil, ½ tsp salt. ½ tsp garlic, and ¼ tsp pepper.   Spread them out evenly on the paper and roast for 15 minutes or until they soften and turn brown.

2. Push your potatoes to one side of the sheet pan and arrange your salmons at the center. Add 1 ½ tsp of minced garlic and 2 tsp of parsley and rub every salmon with the mixture. Add asparagus to the other end of the pan.

3. Return them to the oven and continue baking until your potatoes are fork tender and the salmons are opaque throughout.

4. In a bowl combine lemon juice, garlic, and the remaining butter with wine or chicken stock. Serve your salmon with vegetables and lemon slices.

Nutritional value per serving

Calories 566, Fats 38g, Carbohydrates 19g, Proteins 37g, Sodium: 970 Mg, Potassium: 1549mg.

Shrimp Cakes

Preparation time: 10 minutes cooking time: 15 minutes serves: 3

Ingredients

½ tsp salt

2 eggs

1 tsp lemon zest

¼ teaspoon pepper

¼ cup finely diced red bell pepper

1-pound raw shrimp deveined and peeled

3 tsp chives

Lemon wedges

4 tsp olive oil

Instructions

1. Place the shrimp in a bowl or food processor. pulse them until they are coarsely chopped. Avoid grinding them to paste/

2. Transfer your shrimp into a large bowl and add red bell pepper, chives, panko bread crumbs, salt, eggs, pepper, and lemon zest. Stir them until there are well combined.

3. Form your shrimp mixture into 6 patties, heat the olive oil in a pan over medium heat. Add the shrimp patties in a single layer and cook them for 5 minutes or until you see each side turn golden brown.

4. Serve immediately with sour cream and additional chives. Garnish with lemon wedges.

Nutritional value per serving

Calories 90, Fat 2g, Carbs 7g, Proteins 11g, Sodium: 290mg

Easy Honey Garlic Salmon

Preparation time: 10 minutes cook time: 10 minutes serves: 4

Ingredients

½ test paprika

Salt and pepper

4 wild caught salmon

4 cloves garlic

2 tsp butter

4 cloves garlic minced

4 tsp honey

1 tsp water

2 tsp soy sauce

Lemon wedges

1 tsp freshly squeezed lemon

Instructions

1. Arrange your oven and put it at broil option.
2. Season your salmon with paprika, salt and pepper and set it aside.
3. Heat the butter in a pan over medium heat add your garlic and sauté for a minute. Pour honey, soy sauce and water allow for the flavors to fuse. Add lemon juice and mix them thoroughly.
4. Add your salmon steaks to the sauce and cook each side for 4 minutes. Season it with pepper and salt to taste.
5. To serve your salmon drizzle sauce and squeeze of lemon juice. Serve it over rice and salad or vegetables and salad.

Nutritional value per serving

Calories Fats: 13 g, Carbohydrates: 16g, Proteins: 34g, Sodium: 269mg, Potassium: 855mg

Honey Mustard Salmon in a Foil

Preparation time: 5 minutes cook time: 15 minutes serves: 6

Ingredients

¼ cup whole grain mustard

¼ cup honey

¼ cup butter

2 tsp fresh lemon juice

5 cloves garlic minced

2 tsp mild Dijon mustard

¼ tsp chili powder

2 pounds salmon

Black pepper

2 tsp freshly chopped parsley

Lemon wedges

Instructions

1. Position you are in the middle of the oven. Preheat it to 375 degrees Fahrenheit. Line your baking tray with a piece of foul that is able to fold over and create a packet. You can use two foils depending on the size of the foils on use and size of the salmon.

2. A small pan combines butter, honey, mustard, lemon and garlic. Whisk them properly until you achieve an even mix and ensure that honey has melted into the butter.

3. Place your salmon into the baking tray and pour the mixture over the salmon and use a spoon to spread them over the salmon. Sprinkle 2 tsp of salt and pepper. Fold the size of the foils to cover the salmon.

4. Bake the salmon until it is fully cooked this will take around 10 minutes.

5. Open the foil and be careful of to avoid escaping steam from injuring you. Broil for 3 minutes to caramelize it on the top and garnish it with parsley before serving it immediately with lemon wedges.

Nutritional value per serving

Calories Fat 15g, Carbohydrates 13g, Proteins 30g, Potassium: 771 Mg, Sodium: 250mg.

Teriyaki Glazed Salmon

Preparation time: 5 minutes cook time: 15 minutes serves: 5

Ingredients

¼ cup cooking sake

¼ cup soy sauce

3 tsp brown sugar

2 tsp mirin

1 tsp Japanese rice wine vinegar

1 tsp sesame

½ tsp garlic powder

6 oz skinless salmon fillets

2 cups of broccoli

1 shallot onion stem

1 large courgetti or zucchini

Instructions

1. Combine sake, brown sugar, soy sauce, mirin, garlic powder and vinegar and mix together in a bowl. Mix them properly until the sugar is dissolved. Pour half of the marinade in a small pan and set aside.

2. Rinse and pat dry your salmon with paper towel. Place your salmon fillets in a bowl with teriyaki glaze and allow it to coat properly.

3. Heat oil in a pan over medium heat and fry the two salmon at a time fry for 4 minutes per side.

4. Bring the glaze to your pan and boil over high heat. Lower the heat gently and simmer while you stir occasionally until you see that the glaze is well thickened.\

5. Serve the salmon over steamed vegetables and pour your teriyaki glaze over the top.

Nutritional value per serving

Calories 428 Fat: 24g, Carbohydrates 15g, Proteins 38g

Chapter 6 Snacks and Appetizers

Healthy 2 Ingredient Breakfast Cookies

Preparation: 4 minutes cooking time: 15 minutes serves 1

Ingredients

1 ¾ cup of quick oats

2 large ripe bananas

4 tsp peanut butter

1/3 cup crushed nuts of your choice

½ tsp pure vanilla extract

¼ cup shredded coconut

Instructions

1. Preheat your oven to 350 degrees Fahrenheit.
2. Mash the bananas in a bowl and add the oats and mix them well to combine. Fold any optional add ins such as ¼ cup chocolate chips. You can add honey to taste.
3. Line your baking tray with parchment paper and drop one tsp of cookie dough per cookie into your tray. Press down with a metal spoon into the shape of the cookies.
4. Bake for 20 minutes depending on your oven or cook them until they are golden brown on top.
5. Remove and allow to cool before serving.

Nutritional value per serving

Calories 24 Carbohydrates 5g, Proteins 1g, Calcium: 4mg, Potassium: 29mg.

Grilled Avocado Caprese Crostini

Preparation time: 10 minutes cook time: 20 minutes serves: 2

Ingredients

1 avocado thinly sliced

9 ounces ripened cherry tomatoes

ounces fresh bocconcini in water

2 tsp balsamic glaze

8 pieces Italian baguette

½ a cup basil leaves

Instructions

1. Preheat your oven to 375 degrees Fahrenheit
2. Arrange your baking sheet properly before spraying them on top with olive oil.
3. Bake your item of choice until they are well done or golden brown. Rub your crostini with the cut side of garlic while they are still warm and you can season them with pepper and salt.
4. Divide the basil leaves on each side of bread and top up with tomato halves, avocado slices and bocconcini. Season it with pepper and salt.
5. Broil it for 4 minutes and when the cheese starts to melt through remove and drizzle balsamic glaze before serving.

Nutritional value per serving

Calories 278 Fat 10g, Carbohydrates 37g, Proteins 10g, Sodium: 342 Mg, Potassium: 277mg

Caprese Stuffed Garlic Butter Portobellos

Preparation time: 5 minutes cook time: 10 minutes serves: 6

Ingredients

For Garlic butter

2 tsp of butter

2 cloves garlic 1 tsp parsley finely chopped

For the mushrooms

6 large portobello mushrooms, washed and dried well with paper towel.

6 mozzarella cheese balls thinly sliced

1 cup grape tomatoes thinly sliced

Fresh basil for garnishing

For balsamic glaze

2 tsp brown sugar

¼ cup balsamic vinegar

Instructions

1. Preheat the oven to broil setting on high heat. Arrange the oven shelf and place it in the right direction.

2. Combine the garlic butter ingredients in a small pan and melt until the garlic begins to be fragrant. Brush the bottoms of the mushroom and place them on the buttered section of the baking tray.

3. Flip and brush the remaining garlic over each cap. Fill each mushroom with tomatoes and mozzarella slices and grill until the cheese has melted. Drizzle the balsamic glaze and sprinkle some salt to taste.

4. If you are making the balsamic glaze from scratch, combine the sugar and vinegar in a small pan and reduce the heat to low. Allow it to simmer for 6 minutes or until the mixture has thickened well.

Nutritional value per serving

Calories 101 Fat 5g, Carbohydrates 12g, Proteins 2g, Sodium: 58mg, Potassium: 377 Mg

Cheesy Mashed Sweet Potato Cakes

Preparation time: 10 minutes cook time: 30 minutes serves: 4

Ingredients

¾ cup bread crumbs

4 cups mashed potatoes

½ cup onions

2 cup of grated mozzarella cheese

¼ cup fresh grated parmesan cheese

2 large cloves finely chopped

1 egg

2 tsp finely chopped parsley

Salt and pepper to taste

Instructions

1. Line your baking sheet with foil. Wash, peel and cut the sweet potatoes into 6 pieces. Arrange them inside the baking sheet and drizzle a small amount of oil on top before seasoning with salt and pepper.

2. Cover with a baking sheet and bake it for 45 minutes. once cooked transfer them into a mixing bowl and mash them well with a potato masher.

3. To the sweet potatoes in a bowl add green onions, parmesan, mozzarella, garlic, egg, parsley and bread crumbs. Mash and combine the mixture together using the masher.

4. Put the remaining ¼ cup of the breadcrumbs in a place. Scoop a tsp of mixture into your palm and form round patties around ½ and inch thick. Dredge your patties in the breadcrumbs to cover both sides and set them aside.

5. Heat a tablespoon of oil in a medium nonstick pan. when the oil is hot begin to cook the patties in batches 4 or 5 per session and cook each side for 6 minutes until they turn golden brown. Using a spoon or spatula flip them. Add oil to prevent burning.

Nutritional value per serving

Calories 126, Fat 6g, Carbs 15g, Proteins 3g, Sodium: 400mg

Cheesy Garlic Sweet Potatoes

Preparation time: 10 minutes cook time: 25 minutes serves: 4

Ingredients

Sea salt

¼ cup garlic butter melt

¾ cup shredded mozzarella cheese

½ cup of parmesan cheese freshly grated

4 medium sized sweet potatoes

2 tsp freshly chopped parsley

Instructions

1. Heat the oven to 400 degrees Fahrenheit and brush the potatoes with garlic butter and season each with pepper and salt. Arrange the cut side down on a greased baking sheet until the flesh is tender or they turn golden brown.
2. Remove them from the oven, flip the cut side up and top up with parsley and parmesan cheese.
3. Change the settings of your instant fryer oven to broil and on medium heat add the cheese and melt it. sprinkle salt and pepper to taste. Serve them warm

Nutritional value per serving

Calories Fat 9g, Carbohydrates 13g, Proteins 5g, Potassium: 232mg, Sodium: 252mg

Crispy Garlic Baked Potato Wedges

Preparation time: 5 minutes cook time: 10 minutes serves: 3

Ingredients

3 tsp salt

1 tsp minced garlic

6 large russet

¼ cup olive oil

1 tsp paprika

2/3 finely grated parmesan cheese

2 tsp freshly chopped parsley

Instructions

1. Preheat the oven into 350 degrees Fahrenheit and line the baking sheet with a parchment pepper.

2. Cut the potatoes into halfway length and cut each half in half lengthways again. Make 8 wedges.

3. In a small jug combine garlic, oil, paprika and salt and place your wedges in the baking sheets. Pour the oil mixture over the potatoes and toss them to ensure that they are evenly coated.

4. Arrange the potato wedges in a single layer on the baking tray and sprinkle salt and parmesan cheese if needed. Bake for 35 minutes turning the wedges once half side is cooked.

5. Flip the other side until they are both golden brown.

6. Sprinkle parsley and the remaining parmesan before serving.

Nutritional content per serving

Calories, Fat 6g, Carbs 8g, Proteins 2g, Sodium: 51mg, Potassium: 120mg

Sticky Chicken Thai Wings

Preparation time: 10 minutes cooking time: 30 minutes serves: 6

Ingredients

3 pounds chicken wings removed

1 tsp sea salt to taste

For the glaze:

¾ cup Thai sweet chili sauce

¼ cup soy sauce

4 tsp brown sugar

4 tsp rice wine vinegar

3 tsp fish sauce

2 tsp lime juice

1 tsp lemon grass minced

2 tsp sesame oil

1 tsp garlic minced

Instructions

1. Preheat the oven to 350 degrees Fahrenheit. Lightly spray your baking tray with cooking tray and set it aside. To prepare the glaze combine the ingredients in a small bowl and whisk them until they are well combined. Pour half of the mixture into a pan and reserve the rest.

2. Trim any excess skin off the wing edges and season it with pepper and salt. Add the wings to a baking tray and pour the sauce over the wings tossing them for the sauce to evenly coat. Arrange them in a single layer and bake them for 15 minutes.

3. While the wings are in the oven, bring your glaze to simmer in medium heat until there are visible bubbles.

4. Once the wings are cooled on one side rotate each piece and bake for an extra 10 minutes. Baste them and return them into the oven to allow for more cooking until they are golden brown. Garnish with onion slices, cilantro, chili flakes and sprinkle the remain salt. Serving with glaze of your choice.

Nutritional value per serving

Calories Fat :16g, Carbohydrates 19g, Proteins: 20g, Potassium: 213mg, Sodium: 561mg

Coconut Shrimp

Preparation time: 15 minutes cook time: 15 minutes serves: 6

Ingredients

Salt and pepper

1-pound jumbo shrimp peeled and deveined

½ cup all-purpose flour

For batter:

½ cup beer

1 tsp baking powder

½ cup all-purpose flour

1 egg

For coating:

1 cup panko bread crumbs

1 cup shredded coconut

Instructions

1. Line the baking tray with parchment paper.
2. In a shallow bowl add ½ cup flour for dredging and in another bowl whisk the batter ingredients. The batter should resemble a pancake consistency. If it is too thick add a little mineral or beer whisking in between. In another bowl mix together the shredded coconut and bread crumbs.
3. Dredge the shrimp in flour shaking off any excess before dipping in the batter and coat it with bread crumb mixture. Lightly press the coconut into the shrimp.
4. Place them into the baking sheet and repeat the process until you have several.
5. In a Dutch oven skillet heat vegetable oil until it is nice and hot fry the frozen shrimp batches for 3 minutes per side. Drain them on a paper towel lined plate.
6. Serve immediately with sweet chili sauce.

Nutritional value per serving

Calories Fat 11g, Carbohydrates 46g, Proteins 30g, Sodium: 767mg, Potassium: 345mg

Spicy Korean Cauliflower Bites

Preparation time: 15 minutes cook time: 30 minutes serves: 4

Ingredients

2 eggs

1 lb. cauliflower

2/3 cups of corn starch

2 tsp smoked paprika

1 tsp garlic grated

1 tsp ginger grated

1 lb. panko

1 tsp sea salt

For the Korean barbecue sauce

1 cup ketchup

½ cup Korea chili flakes

½ cup minced garlic

½ cup red pepper

Instructions

1. Cut the cauliflower into small sizes based on your taste and preference.
2. In a small bowl add cornstarch and eggs and mix them until they are smooth.
3. Add onions, garlic, ginger, smoked paprika and coat them with panko.
4. Apply some pressure so that the panko can stick and repeat this with all the cauliflower.
5. Set your vortex pls to 400 degrees Fahrenheit for a half an hour. Line your tray with aluminum foil or parchment paper and use nonstick spray to cover it.
6. When the vortex plus BEEPS 'add food' put your food and set the timer to 30 minutes. Or choose a program that will automatically choose the duration the food will take to cook. In the middle of the cooking the appliance will beep again to indicate turn food. You will take it out and flip it for the other side to cook well.
7. While it is cooking for the second part you can begin preparing your spicy Korean barbecue sauce.
8. Sauté the ingredients and drizzle the oil at the bottom. Fry the garlic for a minute before adding all the remaining ingredients and simmering it for 15 minutes.
9. Keep it warm and serve with your cauliflower bites.

Nutritional value per serving

Calories 118, Fat 2g, Carbs 21g, Proteins 4g, Sodium: 1172mg

Mini Popovers

Preparation time: 10 minutes cook time: 15 minutes serves: 4

Ingredients

1 tsp butter melted

2 eggs at room temperature

1 cup of milk at room temperature

1 cup all-purpose flour

Salt and pepper to taste

Instructions

1. Generously coat a mini popover with nonstick spray.
2. Add all the ingredients to a blender and process it at medium speed.
3. Fill each mold with 2 tsp batter. Place a drip pan at the bottom of the cooking chamber.
4. Using the display panel select AIRFRY and adjust it to 400 degrees Fahrenheit and a time of 20 minutes then touch START.
5. When the display panel indicates 'add food' place the egg bite mold on the lower side of the cooking tray.
6. When the display indicates TURN FOOD. Do not touch anything. When the popovers are brown open the cooking chamber and pierce them to release steam and cook for a minute or so.
7. Serve immediately.

Nutritional value per serving

Calories53, Fat 1g, Carbs 9g, Proteins 2g, Sodium:74mg, Potassium: 26mg

Dehydrated Spiced Cauliflower

Preparation time: 10 minutes cooking time: 60 minutes serves 3

Ingredients

½ tsp nutmeg

2 lb. head of cauliflower

1 tsp olive oil

1 tsp smoked paprika

1 tsp hot sauce

1 tsp lime juice

1 tsp cumin

Instructions

1. Chop the cauliflower into tiny sizes that can fit on your thumb. In your large bowl combine cauliflower and the remaining ingredients and toss to coat them evenly.
2. Divide the cauliflower and make an even layer in a baking tray.
3. Place a drip pan at the bottom of the cooking chamber and insert a tray at the top most position and another at the bottom.
4. Use the display panel and choose DEHYDRATE and adjust the temperature to 130 degrees and touch START.
5. When the dehydration process is over. Press START again and remove the popcorn and serve immediately.

Nutritional value per serving

Calories 30. Fat 2g, Carbs 3g, Proteins 0g.

Instant Vortex Plus Asparagus

Preparation time: 10 minutes cook time: 30 minutes serves: 4

Ingredients

1 tsp extra virgin oil

1 lb. asparagus

½ tsp kosher salt

Salt and pepper to taste.

Instructions

1. Set your instant vortex plus to AIRFRY at 400-degree Fahrenheit.   The preheating process will begin and you can also begin to prepare the asparagus.

2. Cut the woody ends about 2 inches off the bottom of the asparagus and coat them with oil before seasoning with salt and pepper.

3. When the instant vortex is ready carefully open its door and use the silicone mitt to pull the tray before loading the asparagus and closing the door.

4. The appliance will automatically begin the cooking process and it will beep halfway through to allow you to flip the food and allow the asparagus to cook further. Once you have cooked the asparagus and is ready.

5. Serve while hot with a sauce of your choice

Nutritional value per serving

Calories 136 Fat 12g, Carbs 4g, Proteins 3g, Fiber 2g

Roasted Ranch Potatoes

Preparation time: 5 minutes cook time: 15 minutes serves:2

Ingredients

1 tsp olive oil

1 ½ dry ranch seasoning and salad dressing mix

1.5 lbs. of potatoes

Instructions

1. Cut the potatoes into 1-inch chunk, for smaller potatoes you can cut them into quarters.
2. Rinse the potato chunks in cold water and place them in a plate with paper towels. This is effective because it will help in reducing water in the potatoes.   Toss the potatoes in seasoning and preheat your air fryer
3. Once the air fryer has attained the right temperature it is time to load it with the potatoes. Add the potatoes at 380 degrees Fahrenheit.
4. Cook the potatoes for 7 minutes before flipping them and cooking them again for another 7 minutes. Your fryer should be on baking mode.
5. Once the potatoes are golden brown, remove them and serve with a sauce of your choice.

Nutritional value per serving

Calories 231 Fat 7g, Carbs 37, Proteins 5g, Sodium: 660mg

Preparation time: 10 minutes cook time: 40 minutes serves: 4

Ingredients

1 tsp fresh thyme

3 tsp unsalted butter

1 tsp fresh safe

1 tsp fresh rosemary leaves

Fully grated lemon zest

2 tsp kosher salt

2 cloves garlic

Freshly ground pepper

For the gravy

4 tsp unsalted butter

¼ cup all-purpose flour

2 ½ cups chicken broth

Salt and pepper to taste

Instructions

1. Make the turkey by placing 3 tsp of unsalted butter in a bowl and allowing it to melt at room temperature. Prepare 1 Tso fresh thyme leaves, 1 tsp rosemary leaves, 1 tsp sage, 1 tsp grated lemon zest, 2 minced garlic cloves. add a teaspoon of kosher salt and ground black pepper before smashing everything together into a paste.

2. Pat the turkey dry with paper towels before loosening its skin. Spread the butter mixture in an even layer all over the skin of the chicken. Season the turkey with the remaining 1 tsp of kosher salt, and ½ tsp of ground black pepper.

3. Line your baking tray with a parchment paper or a baking sheet. Set the appliance to 350 degrees Fahrenheit and set the cook time to 40 minutes.   Place the turkey skin side down on the rack and push start button on the panel. Allow the turkey to cook for 20 minutes before flipping the other side to cook as well.

4. While the other part of the turkey is cooking make the gravy by melting 4 tsp of unsalted butter in a pan and whisk ¼ cup of flour and cook it for 3 minutes cooking it continuous before adding chicken stock. Simmer until the gravy has thickened well. Taste and season, it with salt and pepper until the turkey is amazing.

5. Serve while hot.

Nutritional value per serving

Calories 296.9 Fat 16.9g, Carbs 3.3g, Proteins 32.9g, Sodium: 407.4mg

Apple Cider Donuts

Preparation time: 25 minutes cook time: 45 minutes serves: 6

Ingredients

3 cups all-purpose flour

2 cups apple cider

½ cup light brown sugar

2 tsp baking powder

1 tsp ground cinnamon

1 tsp ground ginger

8 tsp unsalted butter

½ tsp baking soda

1 tsp kosher salt

For finishing:

¼ cup all-purpose flour

8 tsp unsalted butter

1 cup granulated sugar

1 tsp cinnamon

Instructions

1. Pour 2 cups of apple cider into a pan and bring it to boil transfer the reduced apple dicer once it is half the volume and allow it to cool completely.
2. Put 3 cups all-purpose flour, ½ cup brown sugar, 1 tsp ground cinnamon, 2 tsp baking soda, ½ tsp kosher salt and 1 tsp ground ginger in a bowl and whisk them properly.
3. Grate 8 cold unsalted butter and add it to the mixture using your fingers and incorporate the butter into the dough well. Make it perfect at the center of the mixture and add 1 cup of reduce cider and ½ cup of cold milk as well and use a spatula to mix the dough together.
4. Sprinkle the dough on a surface and have a few table spoons of flour on the surface for shaping the dough. Pat the dough into an even layer about an inch thick and sprinkle more flour. Fold and repeat the procedure again until the dough is less springy. Pat the dough into a 9x13 inch rectangular about ½ inch thick.
5. Cut the donut out of the dough using a floured donut cutter.
6. Transfer your donuts into a baking sheet and gather the scraps before patting the dough again and repeat this process until you have 18 donuts.
7. Preheat your air fryer and put it at 375 degrees Fahrenheit.
8. Melt the remaining butter in a medium pan and add granulated sugar and 1 tsp of ground cinnamon and whisk them together.
9. Depending on the size of the air fryer, you can bake a batch at a time until you have ready donuts. Serve the donuts warm once it is golden brown with warm cider for dipping.

Nutritional value per serving

Calories 322 Fat 12.4g, Carbs 49.1g, Proteins 3.5g, Sodium: 173.8mg

Stuffing hushpuppies

Preparation time: 10 minutes cooking time: 12 minutes serves: 3

Ingredients

A cooking trays

3 cups of cold stuffing

1 large egg

Instructions

1. Place the egg in a large bowl and beat it. Add 3 cups of stuffing and stir until they are well combined.

2. Preheat your instant air fryer to 375 degrees Fahrenheit and set it to 12 minutes.

3. Remove the cooking tray and spray it with a cooking spray before adding the hushpuppies into the racks. Spray on top of the hushpuppies as well. Cook for 6 minutes before flipping.

4. Once you are halfway flip the hushpuppies to allow for the other side to cook well. Repeat this with the remaining hushpuppies.

5. Serve with a sauce of your choice.

Nutritional value per serving

Calories 237.4 Fat 16.6g, Carbs 18.8g, Proteins 3.2g, Sodium :373.3mg

Air Fryer Mozzarella Sticks

Preparation time: 40 minutes cook time: 25 minutes serves: 4

Ingredients

1 package mozzarella sticks cut in half

¼ cup mayonnaise

1 large egg

¼ cup all-purpose flour

¼ cup fine dry breadcrumbs

½ tsp onion powder

½ tsp garlic powder

1 cup marinara sauce

Instructions

1. Before you begin frying have your mozzarella sticks have and on a baking sheet with parchment paper or baking sheet.   Set them to freeze for 30 minutes.
2. Meanwhile you can assemble the breading by whisking mayonnaise and egg together in a bowl and adding bread crumbs, onions, garlic and flour.
3. Work with batches of 6, roll these frozen sticks in the mayo-egg mixture to coat before passing through the flour. Be sure to remove excess flour before putting it in the air fryer.
4. Repeat this procedure until you have several batches of six. Put the appliance on BAKE mode and allow it to attain 370 degrees Fahrenheit. Bake the 6 sticks at a time for 5 minutes and remove them once the panel displays ready. Repeat this with the remaining sticks and serve with warm marinara sauce.

Nutritional content per serving

Calories 253 Fat 22.5g, Carbs 9.0g, Proteins 14.5g, Sodium:503.3mg

Churro Bites with Chocolate Dipping Sauce

Preparation time: 15 minutes cooking time 20 minutes serves: 4

Ingredients

1 cup water

8 tsp unsalted butter

1 cup all-purpose flour

½ cup granulated sugar

1 tsp vanilla extract

3 large eggs

2 tsp of ground cinnamon

4 ounces chopped dark chocolate

¼ cup sour cream

Instructions

1. Bring butter, water and 1 tsp of sugar to boil and allow it to simmer for some minutes. Add the flour quickly and with a sturdy wooden spoon continue to stir until the flour smells like it is toasted. Transfer the mixture into a large bowl.

2. Using the same wooden spoon beat the flour mixture until it is cooled slightly and add vanilla extract. Stir in the eggs one at a time making sure that each egg is well incorporated before adding the next one.

3. Transfer the dough into a zip top bag and let it rest for an hour. In the meantime, prepare cinnamon sugar and chocolate sauce. Combine the cinnamon and remaining ½ cup sugar in a bowl and microwave them for 2 minutes until everything has melted in well. add the sour cream and whisk until it is smooth. Cover and set aside.

4. Preheat your fryer to attain 375 degrees Fahrenheit. Add butter to the preheated fryer and making 6 pieces of ½ inch churros.   Once the appliance has attained the temperature it will prompt you to add the food. Add the food and bake them until they are golden brown. Repeat this for all the pieces that you have.

5. Once ready immediately transfer the churros with cinnamon and sugar to coat them.

Nutritional value per serving

Calories Fat 14.4g, Carbs 26.8g, Proteins 4.3g, Sodium: 26.8mg

Air Fryer Mini Calzones

Preparation time: 25 minutes cook time: 12 minutes serves: 8

Ingredients

1 cup pizza sauce

1-pound pizza dough

All-purpose flour

8 ounces shredded mozzarella cheese

6 ounces sliced pepperoni

Instructions

1. On a lightly floured surface roll your pizza dough until it a quarter inch thick. Use the 3-inch cutter or a glass to cut 10 rounds of the dough and transfer the rounds to a baking sheet lined tray.
2. Gather up the dough scraps and reroll them and gather them and make more rounds.
3. Top each round with 2 tsp of sauce, 1 tsp pepperoni and 1 tsp of cheese. Working with one dough at a time fold them in half and then pinch the edges to seal with each calzone sealed use for to crimp the edges and seal it further.
4. Heat your air fry and put it to 375 degrees Fahrenheit. Once it reaches that temperature it will indicate that it is ready and you should add food. Use the baking tray to put the calzones into the cooking chamber. Cook each batch for 8 minutes or until you see that they have turned golden brown. Repeat this for the remaining pieces.
5. Serve with pizza dipping sauce

Nutritional value per serving

Calories Fat 9.3g, Carbs 16.4g. Proteins 8.4g, Fiber 1.1 G, Sodium: 516.5mg

Air Fryer Beignets

Preparation time: 20 minutes cook time: 28 minutes servs: 3

Ingredients

1 cup plain Greek yoghurt

1 tsp granulated sugar

1 tsp vanilla extract

1 cup self-rising flour

2 tsp unsalted butter

½ cup powdered sugar

Instructions

1. Stir the yoghurt, vanilla, granulated sugar in a medium bowl and add the flour until the flour is moistened and a dough is formed.

2. Turn the dough in a working surface and fold it two or three times until it is smooth. Pat the mixture and make 4x5 inch rectangles cutting the into 9 pieces. Separate these pieces using flour and set aside for 15 minutes.

3. Heat the air fryer to 375 degrees Fahrenheit. in a large baking tray with parchment paper or baking sheet set the pieces apart.

4. Once the appliance has achieved the temperature it will prompt you to add food and this is where you lightly coat the frying basket with olive oil and brush the beignets as well with butter.

5. The side with butter side should face down and close the fryer and cook for 4 minutes before flipping them. Once it is halfway flip them and allow them to cook for another 4 minutes. repeat this procedure for the remaining beignets. Serve them warm with a dipping sauce of your choice.

Nutritional value per serving

Calories Fat 6.8g, Carbs 26.7g, Proteins 4.9g, Fiber 0.6g, Sodium: 266.9mg

Chapter 7 Vegetarian

Garlic Parmesan Mac and Cheese

Preparation time: 10 minutes cooking time: 30 minutes serves: 4

Ingredients

1-pound dry weight macaroni or pasta

Crispy topping

2/3 cup panko breadcrumbs

1 ½ teaspoons butter

For the sauce:

¾ cup low fat grated cheese

1 tsp chicken bouillon powder

¼ cup butter

4 cloves garlic crushed

¼ cup flour

4 ½ cups milk

1 tsp cornstarch

6 ounces mozzarella cheese

1 cup grated parmesan cheese

Instructions

1. Boil the pasta in salted water or as per packet instructions.
2. Preheat your oven to 365 degrees Fahrenheit
3. Melt 2 tsp of butter in a large oven and add the breadcrumbs stir and coat them until they are golden brown. Transfer into a bowl and set aside.
4. Melt ¼ cup of butter in a pan add garlic and sauté until it is fragrant. Whisk some flour and cook while stirring reduce the heat down and add 4 cups of milk/
5. In a separate jug combine ½ cup of milk and corn starch and whisk until it is lump free and stir through the white sauce to thicken. Season with salt and stir the bouillon powder.
6. Remove from the heat and add cheddar, mozzarella slices, and ¾ cup of parmesan cheese. Toss the pasta through the sauce to ensure that they are completely coated.
7. Top up with the panko and remaining parmesan cheese before broiling for about 15 minutes.
8. Allow to cook before serving.

Nutritional content

Calories Fat 17g, Carbohydrates 46g, Proteins 20g, Potassium: 291mg, Sodium; 546mg

Garlic Green Beans with Parmesan

Preparation time: 10 minutes cook time: 20 minutes serves: 3

Ingredients

1 tsp sea salt

1-pound green beans

1 tsp finely chopped garlic

2 tsp olive oil

2 tsp freshly chopped parsley

¼ cup parmesan cheese

Instructions

1. Preheat the oven to 380-degree Fahrenheit. Lightly coat the baking tray with oil spray.
2. Arrange the green beans in one layer. Drizzle oil and season with pepper, salt, garlic and parmesan. Toss the beans to ensure that they are evenly coated.
3. Roast them in the oven for 25 minutes tossing halfway through the cooking time to ensure that they are well cooked.
4. Remove from the oven and season with pepper and salt to taste.
5. Sprinkle over parsley and serve.

Nutritional value per serving

Calories Fat 8g, Carbohydrates 9g, Proteins 4g, Calcium: 122mg, Potassium: 250mg, Sodium: 689mg

Crispy Garlic Baked Potato Wedges

Preparation time: 10 minutes cooking time: 20 minutes serves: 4

Ingredients

2 tsp fresh chopped parsley

2/3 cup grated parmesan

1 tsp paprika

1 tsp minced garlic

¼ cup olive oil

6 large potatoes rinsed

Instructions

1. Preheat the oven to 350 degrees Fahrenheit. Line 2 large parchment papers and set aside.
2. Cut the potato wedges halfway and repeat the process on the other sides until you have 8 wedges.
3. In a small bowl combine salt, garlic, oil and paprika. Place the wedges into the baking sheets. pour the oil mixture over the potatoes and toss them to ensure that they are coated evenly.
4. Arrange the wedges in a layer of baking tray and sprinkle the half parmesan cheese and extra salt if required. Bake for another 30 minutes until the wedges turn golden brown.
5. Sprinkle with parsley and the remaining parmesan cheese before serving.

Nutritional value per serving

Calories, Fat 0g, Carbs 17g, Proteins 2g, Sodium: 200mg

Crispy Parmesan Baked with Veggies

Preparation time: 10 minutes cook time: 25 minutes serves: 4

Ingredients

1 tsp lemon juice

1 large egg

2 tsp minced garlic

½ tsp freshly chopped parsley

½ tsp pepper and salt to season

4 skinless boneless chicken breasts

1/3 cup grated parmesan

½ cup bread crumbs

8 pounds baby potatoes

2 tsp minced garlic ½ cup butter melted

1-pound green beans

Instructions

1. Preheat the oven to 350 degrees Fahrenheit. Lightly grease the baking tray with cooking oil and set aside.
2. In a large bowl whisk lemon, egg, parsley, salt, pepper 2 tsp garlic and mix them thoroughly.
3. Dip the chicken into the egg mixture and cover it to allow to marinate inside the fridge.
4. In another bowl combine the bread crumb with parmesan cheese. Dredge the egg coated with parmesan mixture and lightly press to even coat.
5. Place the chicken in baking sheet and lightly coat it with oil mix the chicken and potatoes in a single layer. Add 2 tsp garlic and salt to test and pour half the mixture over the potatoes and toss to evenly coat.
6. Bake the mixture in a preheated oven. remove the baking tray and flip the chicken breast. Move the potatoes on one side and green beans around the chicken on the other aide. Pour the remaining garlic and butter and set to broil over medium heat for 10 minutes.
7. Sprinkle freshly chopped parsley and serve immediately.

Nutritional value per serving

Calories 494 Fat 22g, Carbohydrates 41 G, Proteins 33g. Sodium: 852mg, Potassium: 1291mg

Chapter8 Side dishes

Orzo Salad

Preparation time: 10 minutes cook time: 10 minutes serves: 6

Ingredients

3 tsp red wine vinegar

3 tsp olive oil

½ tsp dried oregano

½ tsp kosher salt

¼ tsp freshly ground pepper

1 jar marinated artichoke hearts

1 jar roasted red pepper coarsely chopped

½ large English cucumber diced

1 cup pitted kalamata olives

½ cup freshly chopped parsley

6 ounces feta cheese

Instructions

1. Bring a large pot of salted water to boil. Whisk oregano, vinegar, oil, salt and a few grinds of black pepper and set them aside.

2. Add the orzo into the water and cool them for 10 minutes. drain and run briefly through cold water and allow them to cool.

3. Add peppers, cucumbers, artichoke hearts, red onions, and olives in a dressing bowl. Toss them thoroughly to allow them to combine them. add parsley and feta and toss them again. Allow it to sit for 20 minutes before stirring them from time to time to allow the flavors to blend well. Taste and season, it to your liking.

Nutritional value per serving

Calories 305.8 Fat 17g, Carbohydrates 28.9g, Proteins 9.3 g

Fondant Potatoes

Preparation time: 10 minutes cook time: 45 minutes serves: 6

Ingredients

3 cloves garlic

4 medium potatoes

4 tsp unsalted butter

½ tsp kosher salt

½ tsp freshly ground pepper

¾ cup low sodium vegetable broth

4 sprigs fresh thyme

Instructions

1. Peel the russet potatoes, trim the ends, and cut each potato into half. You should have 8 flat potato rounds. Put the potatoes in a large bowl and cover them with cold water. Allow it to sit for 20 minutes at room temperature to allow excess starch to be removed. Heat the oven and prepare butter and garlic.

2. Arrange a rack in the middle of the oven and heat it to 350 degrees Fahrenheit. Lightly smash and peel the 3 garlic cloves. Cut 4 tsp unsalted butter into 8 pieces.

3. Drain the potatoes and rise it with cold water. Pat them dry with paper towels. season the potatoes with ½ tsp black pepper and ½ tsp of kosher salt.

4. Heat 2 tablespoons of canola oil in a large oven and then add your potatoes cut side down in a single layer. Put them inside the oven and cook until they are brown. You will see the panel indicating that TURN FOOD.

5. When your instant fryer indicates this message flip the potatoes using tongs and add butter, garlic and 4 sprigs thyme and allow them to cook for 3 minutes. Cook until the butter begins to foam, then add ¾ cup vegetable broth.

6. Bake your potatoes until they are fork tender and slightly browned on the sides. This should take around 30 minutes, garnish with thyme sprigs before serving them drizzled with juices from your oven pan.

Nutritional value per serving

Calories 180.4, Fat 9.6g, Carbohydrates 20.5g, Protein 3.0 g, Sodium: 156.1 Mg

Leftover Mashed Potato Pancakes

Preparation time: 20 minutes cook time: 10 minutes serves:3

Ingredients

1 large egg

1-ounce parmesan cheese

2 tsp chopped fresh chives

2 cups cold mashed potatoes

½ cup all-purpose flour

2 tsp olive oil

Sour cream for serving

Instructions

1. Grate an ounce of parmesan cheese and place it in a large bowl. Chop fresh chives until you have 2 tsps. Add one large egg and beat them with a wooden spoon to combine. Divide the potato mixture into 8 portions. Here you will work with one at a time.

2. Shape each portion into a patty around 3 inches diameter then dredge both sides into ¼ cup all-purpose flour. Shake of the excess and place them in a large baking sheet.

3. Heat the remaining olive oil in a baking try and using a wide spatula transfer the patties and allow them to cook. Press START on the panel and allow the food to cook. When the panel indicates TURN FOOD, flip the patties and allow the other side to cook.

4. Serve them warm with sour cream.

Nutritional value per serving

Calories 299.2, Fat 15.2g, Carbohydrates 30.3g, Protein 10.3 g, Fiber 2.0g, Sodium: 582.9mg.

Classic Corn Bread Dressing

Preparation: 20 minutes cook time; 45 minutes serves: 7

Ingredients

2 cups diced white onion

1 recipe whole grain corn bread

1 ½ cups diced celery

2 tsp parsley finely chopped

2 tsp fresh sage leaves

¼ cup flat leaf parsley

3 tsp canola oil

2 large eggs

1 tsp freshly ground black pepper

Cooking spray

½ tsp kosher salt

Instructions

1. Arrange your rack in the middle and heat the oven to 360 degrees Fahrenheit. Meanwhile be preparing 2 cups white onions, 1 ½ cup celery, finely chopped fresh sage leaves and put them in the same bowl. Coarsely chop until you have a ¼ cup of parsley leaves.

2. Heat 3 tsp canola oil over medium heat until it shimmers. Add onion, celery and cook while stirring until they are tender, this should take around 10 minutes. Add sage, thyme, 1 tsp black pepper, ½ tsp kosher salt and cook until fragrant. Remove from the heat and let it cool slowly.

3. Coat a low ceramic baking dish with cooking oil. Crumble cornbread in a large bowl. Beat two eggs, add the eggs to an onion mixture, 2 ½ cups of chicken stock and stir well for them to combine well. Transfer the mixture into a baking dish.

4. Put your instant air fryer into baking mode and press start. Baking until the dressing is lightly browned this is about 45 minutes. You can cover with an aluminum foil to prevent the mixture from being too browned.

5. Allow it to cook for 10 minutes before serving it.

Nutritional value per serving

Calories 260.6, Fat 11 g, Carbohydrates 31.2 g, Proteins 9.2 g, Sodium: 421.6g.

Roasted Brussels Sprouts with Ginger and Scallions

Preparation time: 10 minutes cook time: 25 minutes serves: 4

Ingredients

3 tsp olive oil

10 medium scallions

2 tsp peeled grated ginger

1-pound Brussel sprouts

1 tsp low sodium soy sauce

½ tsp kosher salt

Freshly ground pepper

Instructions

1. Put your instant air fryer oven on and arrange a rack in the middle of the oven. Allow it to gain temperature until it attains 380 degrees Fahrenheit. When it is ready place a parchment paper or baking sheet in the oven tray and trim half of the 1-pound Brussel sprouts.

2. Trim your scallions and cut them into ½ inch pieces, peel and mince them until you have 2 tsp of ginger.

3. Place the brussels sprouts and scallions on the baking sheet. Season with ginger and 3 tsp of olive oil, 1 tsp of low sodium soy sauce, ½ tsp kosher salt and a generous grind of black pepper.

4. Arrange the Brussel sprouts in a single layer cut side facing down. Bake them for 15 minutes or until the panel display TURN FOOD, flip them and allow the other side to cook as well. Once cooked the air fryer will go on standby mode. Taste and season with more sauce if you need.

Nutritional value per serving

Calories 168.2 Fat 10.6g, Carbs 13.5g, Proteins 4.7g, Sodium: 310.4 Mg

Bagna Cauda Roasted Brussels Sprouts

Preparation time: 10 minutes cook time: 25 minutes serves: 4

Ingredients

4 anchovies

8 cloves garlic

¼ cup olive oil

8 tsp unsalted butter

½ tsp kosher salt

1-pound Brussel sprouts

Freshly ground pepper

Instructions

1. Put your oven on and put on baking mode on. Allow it to attain temperature of 380 degrees Fahrenheit. Meanwhile peal and thinly slice your garlic cloves. Rinse and pat your anchovies with paper towels and mince them. Place the anchovies and garlic in a small pan and add 1 stick of unsalted butter and ¼ cup of olive oil and simmer the Brussel sprouts until they are almost ready.

2. Trim and have the Brussel sprouts, place them in a hot baking sheet. Season the remaining ½ tsp kosher salt, 3 tsp olive oil, a generous grind of black pepper and toss them to combine fully. Arrange the Brussel sprouts in a single layer, cut side down.

3. Bake them for 15 minutes or until the panel indicates TURN FOOD, flip them and allow them to cook on the other side as well.

4. Once done, transfer the Brussel sprouts to a serving bowl and add Bagna cauda before tossing them and serving them.

Nutritional value per serving

Calories 499, Fat 47.4g, Carbohydrates 12.5 G, Proteins 5.6g, Sodium: 409.2mg

Indian-ish Baked Potatoes

Preparation time: 10 minutes cook time: 45 minutes serves: 4

Ingredients

¼ cup sour cream

1-pound baby red potatoes

2 tsp kosher salt

½ small red onion finely diced

4 tsp minced ginger

2 small Indian chilies

2 tsp chaat masala

2 tsp chopped fresh cilantro

Instructions

1. Preheat your oven to 400 degrees Fahrenheit. Peel and wash or just wash your baby potatoes and put them in a baking tray. Turn the baking mode on the instant air fryer.   Bake them for 45 minutes or until they are fork tender. Allow them to cook until you are satisfied with the level.

2. Without cutting all the way to the bottom part, slice each potato into 4 sections. Use your hands to pull apart and push the four sections to make something like a blooming flower.

3. Sprinkle a pinch of salt in each potato before adding a tablespoon of sour cream. Evenly divide the onions, ginger, green chilies and chaat masala among the potatoes. Add chopped cilantro and serve while hot.

Nutritional value per serving

Calories 128.3, Fat 3.1g, Carbs 22.3g, Proteins 2.8g, Sodium: 15.2mg

Maple-Roasted Delicata Squash with Bacon

Preparation time: 10 minutes cook time: 25 minutes serves: 4

Ingredients

2 slices thick cut bacon

1 tsp olive oil

2 medium Delicata squash

1 tsp pure Marple syrup

Freshly ground black pepper

Kosher salt

Chopped parsley leaves

Instructions

1. Put your instant air fryer on bake mode and allow it to attain 375 degrees Fahrenheit.
2. Trim 2 medium Delicata squash, cutting each half lengthwise and scrapping of the seeds and pulp.
3. Slice into ¼ inch and placed them in a rimmed parchment paper or a baking sheet. Cut 2 slices of bacon and add them into the baking sheet.
4. Drizzle the bacon and squash with 1 tsp olive oil and 1 tsp maple syrup. Season it with salt and pepper then toss them before spreading into an even.
5. Bake them for some time until the air fryer indicates TURN FOOD, flip them and allow the other side to cook as well. Once it is well done garnish with chopped parsley if that is what you like.

Nutritional value per serving

Calories 205 Fat 9.4 G, Carbohydrates 26.5g, Proteins 3.6g, Sodium:103.3 g

Brussels Sprouts with Bacon

Preparation time: 10 minutes cook time: 25 minutes serves: 4

Ingredients

¼ cup olive oil

2 pounds Brussel sprouts

¼ tsp red pepper flakes

Freshly ground black pepper

2 tsp freshly squeezed lemon

4 sliced uncured bacon

¼ cup freshly grated parmesan cheese

Instructions

1. Put your vortex air instant fryer to bake mode and allow it to gain temperature until 380 degrees Fahrenheit.   Meanwhile remove outer leaves and any undesired items from the 2 pounds of Brussel sprouts before trimming the ends.   Keep the tiny ones as a whole and trim the large ones.

2. Put your Brussels in a parchment paper or rimmed baking sheet. Add ¼ cup of olive oil and season it with ½ tsp salt, black pepper and ¼ tsp red pepper flakes.   Toss them and arrange them in a single layer on a baking tray.

3. Bake until the sprouts are lightly brown or until the panel indicates TURN FOOD, bake them until they turn crispy or brown to your liking.   Cook the grated cheese and bacon in a pan and allow the cheese to melt before flipping. Transfer to a paper towel lined plate and grate ¼ cup parmesan cheese.

4. Transfer your Brussel sprouts into a serving bowl and drizzle with 2 tablespoons of lemon juice and toss them to combine. Taste before seasoning with salt and pepper to your liking.

Nutritional value per serving

Calories 241.4 Fat 17.0g, Carbohydrates 14.5g, Proteins 7.6g, Sodium: 357.1 Mg

Garlic Parmesan Monkey Bread

Preparation time: 30 minutes cook time: 25 minutes serves: 4

Ingredients

4 tsp unsalted butter

1-pound pizza dough

2 tsp olive oil

4 cloves garlic minced

½ tsp dried basil

½ tsp dried parsley flakes

½ tsp dried oregano

½ cup freshly grated parmesan cheese

Kosher salt

Instructions

1. Coat an 8X5 inch pan with cooking oil. Cut the pizza dough into 1-ounce pieces and form each piece into a ball.
2. Stir your butter, oil, basil, garlic, oregano, and salt in a bowl. Add the dough ball into the bowl and toss them until they are well coated. Stack the dough balls in a pan and make 2 layers of 8 dough balls on each end.
3. Pour the remaining butter mixture over the dough, cover with a plastic wrap and set it in a warm spot to allow rising.
4. Put your instant air fryer oven into baking mode and allow it to attain the right temperature of 350 degrees Fahrenheit.
5. Uncover and sprinkle them with parmesan. Put them in the oven and bake them until they are golden brown at the center. Once done the panel will indicate the same. Remove and cool them in a rack. Invert the place and serve warm.

Nutritional value per serving

Calories 543.9, Fats 27.5g, Carbohydrates 58.7g, Proteins 15.4g, Sodium 893.3mg, Fibers 3.2g

Grilled Crash Potatoes

Preparation time: 10 minutes cook time: 40 minutes serves: 4

Ingredients

1 lemon halved

1 tsp kosher salt

1 ½ pounds red potatoes

3 tsp olive oil

½ tsp freshly ground pepper

1 clove garlic minced

2 tsp mayonnaise

2 stalks celery

½ thinly sliced shallot

Fresh chives and parsley

Instructions

1. Put your potatoes and a tablespoon of salt in a large pan and add enough cold water to cover them.   Bring them to boil over high heat and reduce the heat and simmer until the potatoes can be pierced with a knife.
2. Meanwhile heat your oven frill to 380 degrees Fahrenheit. Dry your potatoes and place a parchment paper on a baking pan.   Toss the potatoes with ¼ tsp pepper, ¾ tsp salt. Transfer the potatoes into a baking sheet and use a potato masher to flatten the potatoes to an inch thick.
3. Clean your oven and put the potatoes on the oven and allow them to bake until they are golden brown. Once the appliance indicates turn food. Flip them and allow the other side to cook as well until they are crispy and golden brown.
4. Whisk garlic, mayonnaise, paprika and the remaining ¼ tsp pepper, ¼ tsp salt and 1 tsp lemon juice in a large bowl.
5. Arrange your potatoes, shallots, celery, and grilled lemons in halves in a serving plate. Drizzle the dressing on top and sprinkle some herbs. Serve while hot.

Nutritional value per serving

Calories 187.5, Fat 10.7g, Carbohydrates 20.3g, Proteins 2.5g, Sodium: 354mg.

Avocado Salad

Preparation time: 10 minutes cook time: 25 minutes serves: 4

Ingredients

½ small red onion

1-pint cherry tomatoes

2 medium avocados

½ medium English cucumber chopped

¼ tsp kosher salt

2 tsp olive oil

¼ tsp freshly ground black pepper

Instructions

1. Place your tomatoes, avocado, onion, cucumber and herbs in a large bowl. Squeeze lemon juice over the top and drizzle some oil. Gently toss them to combine well. Add salt and pepper and toss them some more to gel perfectly.

Nutritional value per serving

Calories 272.2, Fat 21.8g, Carbohydrates 15.7g, Proteins 3.3g Fiber 8.7g, Sodium: 130.9mg

CPSIA information can be obtained
at www.ICGtesting.com
Printed in the USA
LVHW060836121020
668068LV00056B/49